THE
PEOPLE
OF
GOD

Spence Shelton and Trevor Joy are two of the brightest young stars in the pastoral firmament. In *The People of God: Empowering the Church to Make Disciples* they offer churches a paradigm for discipleship that is both theologically sound and practically helpful. It offers a biblically and theologically driven methodology which centers on the gospel and which takes seriously the high calling of teaching and leading. I recommend it highly as the single-best resource of its type.

—Bruce Ashford
Provost and Dean of Faculty
Southeastern Baptist Theological Seminary

Trevor and Spence are two exceptional leaders who have a passion for discipleship through biblical community. They are gifted leaders in thriving churches who bear the joys and scars of vibrant ministries. As such, they speak with insight and wisdom, which is why I am so thrilled they have written *The People of God*. Read it slowly, digest it completely and you will be challenged by it immensely.

—Bill Willits
Executive Director of Ministry Environments
North Point Ministries and coauthor of *Creating Community*

Few books establish theological foundations, share real-life stories, and give practical direction. This one does all of these while reminding the small group community that it's not about acquiring more church members, it's about making disciples.

—Rick Howerton
Discipleship and Small Group Specialist
LifeWay Christian Resources

TREVOR JOY / SPENCE SHELTON

THE PEOPLE OF GOD

EMPOWERING THE CHURCH TO MAKE DISCIPLES

B&H
PUBLISHING GROUP
NASHVILLE, TENNESSEE

978-1-4336-8370-1

Published by B&H Publishing Group
Nashville, Tennessee

Dewey Decimal Classification: 262
Subject Heading: CHURCH \ DISCIPLESHIP \
CHRISTIAN LIFE

1 2 3 4 5 6 7 8 • 18 17 16 15 14

ACKNOWLEDGMENTS

From Spence Shelton:

To the Summit family, I'm forever grateful to God for how you've lived these pages. To my pastor and friend J.D. Greear, anything good in here I owe to your influence. To Courtney, you are God's grace to me. To Zeke, Ben, Ellie, and Haddie: may you find salvation in Christ, friendship through Christ, and a mission for Christ.

From Trevor Joy:

Thank you to my bride and best friend, Rachel, and our sweet gifts of grace, Addison, Benjamin, and Everett. Thank you to my papaw J.C. Davis, for being an example of godliness. Thank you to John Kerr, the original warrior poet.

To the most ferocious crew of men I know who have taught me the power of biblical community, Josh Patterson,

Matt Chandler, Michael Bleecker, Jason Holleman, thank you.

Finally, thank you to The Village Church staff. What a joy it is to serve alongside a group of men and women so devoted to the kingdom of God.

CONTENTS

FOREWORD

God and God alone saved me; I don't believe one can argue biblically otherwise. He came and rescued me, pulled me out of my sin, and placed my feet on the rock of grace. The means by which He accomplished my salvation was the life, death, and resurrection of Jesus Christ. I have, by the power of the Holy Spirit, sought to know Jesus, follow Jesus, submit to Jesus, and love Jesus ever more deeply for more than twenty years now. As I look back at my conversion, I marvel at the fact that it was very much a community project. Although it was God who saved me with the gospel, the gospel was administered to my soul through the testimonies, encouragements, and friendship of others. It was Jeff Faircloth that shared the good news with me and took me to church, and it was Jerry Hendrix that encouraged me that it was all true. Marcie Hawkins gave me a mix tape with some "Christian" music she thought I would like, and Chris Bryan would always ask me what I was thinking. Although God alone saved me, He used this community of friends to administer the gospel by the power of the Holy Spirit.

My relationship with God in Christ is tremendously personal. I spend time in prayer and contemplation alone. I study the Scriptures for the most part in the quiet spots of my study and dining room table before the kids wake up. I try to pray to the Lord in my head throughout the day, before meetings, in meetings, before I study, while I study, as I workout, for those who are around me as I walk through my day. On a good day I have an ongoing conversation with the sovereign King of the universe. My relationship with God is personal (I can't stress this enough), but it is not and should not be private. Deep, authentic, and honest relationships are imperative to our development, our ongoing maturation in Christ. The more isolated, hidden, and private your relationship with Christ is the more you will be stunted in your ability to grow into all that God has for you in Christ. To state it simply, discipleship is a community project.

Sanctification is the process in which we are being made more and more into the image of Christ. Sanctification can be amazing as we are encouraged and life is spoken into us. It can also be painful as our weakness is brought to our attention. The only way that sanctification can work at full power is for us to be *fully* known. To be 99 percent known is to be unknown. It's hard to be encouraged if we are not known well enough for people to see and know we need it. In the same way we all walk with certain blind spots, areas where we are immature and don't know it, only walking in community will bring those things into the light for us. To be isolated is to willingly hinder your growth into the joy of all that was purchased for you on the cross.

To take this a step further, think about the implications of this for a local church. If the people of a local church are not committed to the communal aspect of the Christian life, if they won't risk being fully known but rather pretend to be more than they are, avoid the deeper parts of life together and instead stay on the surface, then the whole Church becomes immature and the witness of the Church in the world suffers. Grace compels us to be known because God has already outed us as sinners on the cross. The world may hide their weaknesses, but for those of us who believe, we should be in the constant rhythm of confession and repentance. A church full of communities that laugh, cry, pray, eat, confront, and encourage one another will be a power force in the community in which it resides as it reflects the power of the gospel to cover all our sins past, present, and future and celebrates the ongoing work of the Spirit in our lives.

These communities usually are formed organically as people press into knowing Jesus and walking in obedience. One of our jobs as ministers is to encourage these communities and, as best we can, build structures that support them. The most popular way over the last twenty years for these communities to be formed is in what are called "small groups" or "home teams" or some variation of those terms. However we encourage and build structures, we must be careful with whom we encourage to lead these smaller communities of men and women. The Bible makes it clear that, as pastors, we will be held accountable for how we lead, love, protect, and shepherd the people who sit under our care. If we are asking people to be willing to share the joys and pains of their lives, then the people who are put in place to strengthen and foster these communities must be mature and trustworthy. To put it bluntly, the bar of leadership for these organized communities should be high.

I am excited about the book that you are holding in your hand. Both Trevor and Spence are biblically serious and have experience encouraging, organizing, and building group life at church plants and at some of the largest churches in the United States. They are aware of the difficulties at both the leadership level as well as the challenges that exist in helping people believe that the space is a safe place to be known. Praying that the Church is strengthened and encouraged by *The People of God*.

Christ is All,

Matt Chandler

INTRODUCTION

"I like your Christ, I do not like your Christians.
They are so unlike your Christ."
<small>ATTRIBUTED TO MAHATMA GHANDI</small>

What happened?

On a fairly typical Sunday morning in our fairly typical stained-glass-windowed Baptist church, our pastor was halfway through the sermon. At this particular moment he was reading from 1 Timothy. Suddenly a voice from the back shouted, "I resent that!" I (Trevor) was sitting with the youth group (up in the front where we couldn't get in trouble) and we all turned and looked for the speaker.

You have to understand how bizarre this was. At our church, typically there was never an "amen" or any participation whatsoever during the pastor's message. Someone shouting during a sermon in this church would be as out of place and discomforting as someone shouting at actors during a quiet moment at a live theater performance on Broadway.

We scanned the rear to no avail for the shouter and returned our attention to the front, much more attentive to the pastor, who briefly paused. What had he said? Wasn't he just reading the Bible? Maybe I misheard. We didn't have Twitter yet, or I'm sure we'd have confirmed the content of the shout via 48 messages in 10 seconds or less.

Not two minutes later the voice erupted again, "I resent that!" this time followed with "And it's high time you got out of my church!" This time the culprit revealed himself. Roughly 140 heads simultaneously whipped around to see an older man, not only standing, but walking toward the stage to continue voicing his offense at our pastor. I knew the shouter (after all, everybody knew everybody in that church), but I'd never seen him like this. Mad, real mad.

The next 30 seconds seemed like an hour. I'm pretty sure thunder and lightning boomed and a dark cloud began circling overhead as the battle lines for this little steeple-topped battlefield were drawn. A choir robe-clad man shouted from the choir, "Deacons, y'all get this guy outta here."

My mom, who was across the aisle from me, jumped up in support of the surprised and now silent pastor. Then others popped tall after her. The standing people began singing (yes, *singing*) an old hymn I'd never heard called "Onward, Christian Soldiers." I found myself wondering what was going to happen next in this bizarro church moment. Would my Sunday school teacher start reciting the Lord's Prayer from the baptistery? Maybe the pianist would start pounding communion shots?

A couple of men, I presume deacons, physically escorted Old Man Shouter from the room. What happened next was what struck me so deeply. Roughly half of the people in the sanctuary got up and followed the man out. Half of my friends in the youth group followed suit as their parents motioned them to leave. Church attendance just dropped 50 percent mid service! To his credit the pastor had remained silent the entire time and after the chaos, finished his sermon with a heavy, solemn voice.

Per our humdrum Sunday routine, we left at the end of the service and went home. It was one of the last services my family ever attended at that church. The church had become divided like a bad marriage. The "side" that got up and left that day ended up forcing the pastor's resignation and the "side" in support of the pastor mostly left for good. My childhood church had exploded in front of my eyes, in less than one minute.

Was Ghandi right?

For years, Ghandi's words became my modus operandi. Why was the church so messed up? If the early church fathers had been in the room, what would they have said? Where was the joy and generosity the book of Acts talks about? What had we become? Whatever it was, it wasn't church.

We were created for community, and community is redemptive. If the bride of Christ is functioning as He designed us to, we can be a deep, life-giving community and that community *runs* to restore what is broken. Instead of disunity, conflict, and pain, we can dwell together in unity, joy, and redemption.

We have written this book in an attempt to show from Scripture what healthy church life looks like. This book is fueled by a mission we are giving our lives to: to help local churches recover healthy biblical community. We really do believe it can happen and is happening already in many places around the world. We believe church should not be painful or mind numbingly boring. We believe it can be a thrilling, life-giving community, because you were designed by a life-giving three-in-one God for life-giving relationships with others.

Our role as pastors and leaders in the church is to equip and serve our people to be the church to one another. From discipline to benevolence—through equipping our leaders to shepherd well—we continue to push ministry down to where it belongs. There is no substitute for the body being the body!

The people of God should play a primary role in discipleship, and community is the primary context where that discipleship takes place. So you need to declare something right here and right now before you get into chapter 1. You are about to go through church-life recovery. So repeat it with me, out loud like members of a recovery group: "I do not have to settle."

When it comes to the mission God has given to the Church, namely making disciples, you do not have to settle for humdrum church life. The Church is a miraculous movement of God that you and I get to be swept up in. Let's return the mission of God to the people of God. Let's empower the Church to make disciples.

CHAPTER 1

THE SHEPHERD-LEADER

*"I define spiritual leadership as knowing where God
wants people to be and taking the initiative to use
God's methods to get them there in reliance on God's
power. The answer to where God wants people to be
is in a spiritual condition and lifestyle that display
his glory and honor his name. Therefore, the goal of
spiritual leadership is that people come to know God
and to glorify him in all that they do. Spiritual leadership is aimed not so much at directing people as it is
at changing people. If we would be the kind of leaders
we ought to be, we must make it our aim to develop
persons rather than dictate plans. You can get people
to do what you want, but if they don't change in their
heart you have not led them spiritually. You have not
taken them to where God wants them to be."*

JOHN PIPER[1]

When I look at the collegiate generation, I see a vigorous
faith, a willingness to cast everything aside to push a cause

forward. One of my favorite biographies is about a group of college students who caught a fire for something, and it changed the trajectory of their lives. In England during the late 1800s, there was a famous cricket player—yes, cricket—named C. T. Studd.[2] In the cricket world, he would have been considered a top recruit; he was known for his success in the sport all throughout Great Britain.

When Charles was a young man, his father came to faith at a Moody evangelistic campaign sweeping through western Europe. A wealthy and well-known businessman, Charles's father often invited missionaries to stay in his home while on furlough from the field. During one of these stays, the visiting pastor and Charles struck up a series of conversations that led Charles to profess faith in Christ, and the trajectory of this well-known athlete's life changed dramatically.

Not long after, Charles formed a morning Bible study and accountability group with six other men on their college campus, and God began to stir within this community in a powerful way. The most pivotal moment came when a famous missionary to China, Hudson Taylor, gave the chapel message at their college campus, speaking about all God was doing to reach the people of the East. Convicted and ignited, these seven men decided to abandon everything to take the gospel to China.

Prior to leaving for the mission field, they toured several surrounding college campuses, sharing the gospel and God's heart for the nations, and in a powerful movement God ignited missionaries across the country. They were dubbed the "Cambridge Seven," and their influence spread beyond England and even to the US, where it inspired Robert Wilder's Student Volunteer Movement. The Cambridge Seven went on to spend their lives spreading the gospel in some of the hardest and most unreached places of the world.

It began with a small group of seven young men praying and sharing their lives together, and God used that group to spark a gospel journey that took the good news of Jesus Christ across the globe. There were no programs or grandiose initiatives, just the gospel taking root in such a powerful way that it burst into a contagious movement that spread out of the local community and into the world.

The interesting thing about this story is that it is not unique. In fact, this is how the Church has always existed and moved in the world. *This is the normative flow of the gospel among the people of God.* Throughout the New Testament, the Holy Spirit comes upon a people and the gospel takes root in such a way that it transforms that community and begins to flow beyond that group to the world around them (Acts 2:42–47; 2 Cor. 5:16–21). All of us who today claim faith in Jesus Christ are a part of this gospel flow. God used someone to save a man in Wichita Falls, Texas, who then shared the gospel with my brother, who then came home to Dallas and shared it with me. *The mission of God pushes forward through the people of God.*

This is why when we talk about building toward gospel-centered community, we must talk about leaders. If our desire is to see the message of the gospel go forward and transform the hearts and lives of the people in our churches, to spread out in a gospel movement, then we must pay greater attention to the messenger. The simple message of the gospel is that through Christ, God redeems and reconciles your heart and mine to Himself. This message then goes forward through the imperfect and broken vessels in whom it takes root. In his book on building a small groups ministry, C. J. Mahaney says, "The best thing a leader has to offer their group is their own passionate pursuit of God."[3]

There is such beauty and simplicity around how God has designed the Church to advance the Kingdom, one heart at a time. In Matthew 28, Jesus gives marching orders to the Church when He says, *"All authority in heaven and on earth has been given to me.* **Go** *therefore and* **make disciples of all nations**, *baptizing them in the name of the Father and of the Son and of the Holy Spirit,* **teaching them to observe** *all that I have commanded you. And behold,* **I am with you** *always, to the end of the age"* (Matt. 28:18–20; emphasis added). Jesus didn't say, "Go therefore and serve snacks" or "Go therefore and make friends"; He said, "Go therefore and make *disciples*."

When considering all the issues facing pastors and group life among churches across the nation, two problems almost always arise in the conversation around building a healthy group life. First, there are never enough leaders to keep up with demand. A closely related problem is that groups rarely want to multiply and create new groups. We contend that these two problems are symptomatic of a larger issue, a breakdown that has less to do with branding and buy-in than it does with the discipleship culture in your church.

The flow of a gospel-driven community is made up of disciples who make disciples who make disciples. When churches continue to minimize the expectations of leaders and make the barrier of entry into that role as low as possible, the flow decreases.

SHEPHERDS, NOT FACILITATORS

The depth and direction of group ministries will rise and fall depending on the men and women to whom you give the responsibility of leading week in and week out. When we create a low threshold of entry into group leadership, we communicate that we place a low value on the role of leader.

But the importance you place on the role at the front end will affect what the leader accomplishes at the back end.

There is a common denominator that connects every small group. No matter in what church, denomination, country, or context the group exists, all groups share one aspect in common: they are made up of people. Thus, leading a group is going to be messy work, simply because it involves dealing with people! The messiness can be avoided to a degree, but at some point sin and suffering will become apparent in the community, and the leader will have to navigate the deep waters of struggle.

Using a catchy pitch to recruit leaders, telling them that all they will have to do is "facilitate conversation," only sets your leaders up for frustration, and it does not answer the question of how we faithfully care for the people God has entrusted to us. In fact, the term "facilitator" means someone who *makes a process easy.* There is nothing easy about sanctification because it is the deep, arduous, heart-level work of the Holy Spirit transforming us more into the image of Jesus.

The Bible describes the process in terms of grinding off rough edges (Prov. 27:17), breaking bones (Ps. 51:8), and running a long race (Heb. 12:1). There is no way to make sanctification easy, thus the role of a group leader isn't easy. The leader must be a shepherd, not a facilitator. Shepherds don't avoid or manipulate difficult circumstances. They walk faithfully through them. This is the imagery of the Bible, on which Geoff Ashley sheds light:

> Abel was a shepherd, as was Abraham, Jacob and David, just to name a few of the Old Testament figures with such responsibility. God Himself is called a Shepherd in a number of significant passages (Ps. 23), which consequently refer to His people as sheep.
>
> Within the pages of the New Testament, the picture continues as Jesus calls His apostles to be shepherds of the church. (John 21) The apostles then give this charge to the elders (1 Pet. 5:2) of local churches who apparently appoint various shepherds within the congregation. (Eph. 4:1)
>
> While certain positions (pastors, group leaders, etc.) carry an inherent responsibility to guard the flock, everyone in some sense functions as a shepherd.[4]

We are all called to *shepherd* one another at some level. This is what Dietrich Bonheoffer refers to when he writes, "The Christian needs another Christian who speaks God's Word to him."[5] We, as a community of faith, are called to encourage and exhort one another toward greater maturity in Christ. For the purposes of our conversation here, we will stick to the context of shepherding in the local church as a means to being a faithful expression of the body of Christ. There isn't progress, and there is never maturity, without struggle. As the writer of Ecclesiastes puts it, "It is better to go to the house of mourning than to go to the house of feasting, for this is the end of all mankind" (Eccles. 7:2). There is a deeper level of existence to be had when we embrace the reality that our primary reason for gathering and relating to one another is our need for Christ.

Tim Keller says that beneath every sin is an idol, and beneath every idol is a disbelief in the gospel at some level.[6] A healthy biblical community isn't without struggle and strife, but it has the gospel as its centerpiece and axis. The gospel frees us up from the fear of jumping into the deep end because we are afraid we can't swim. The gospel is our buoy of faith in those waters. The gospel frees us up from overprogramming and overcontrolling spiritual formation in the life of our church because all of the promises of the gospel are toward our formation. "He will surely finish what He started," serves as an anchor to those who by faith cling to the redeeming work of the cross.

What does this mean for group leaders and group life? This means that if we are going to experience true gospel transformation in our churches and cities, then we need to start putting our time and attention toward the investments that are going to have the highest rate of return. A catchy phrase or program will never communicate a desire for life change at the same level as the testimony of a transformed life.

So if, while recruiting group leaders, you spend the bulk of your time convincing potential leaders that the water really isn't that deep, you will get people who never want to leave the kiddy pool. The water may be deep, murky, and scary, but the gospel is sufficient for every circumstance that might arise while leading a group of people. If we communicate a passive form of group leadership, we will reap the fruit of passive discipleship.

The job of a leader is to shepherd, not to make the process easy; it is to guide, direct, provide, and care for those on the journey. In the next section we will get to the practical nuts and bolts of who a shepherd-leader is (anatomy) and what they do (function). Don't miss this: we can't keep standing at the edge of this cliff, admiring the view, if we want to mine the riches we have been hoping for in Christ's community. We have to dive off into the depths of all that is difficult and messy. This is the context of discipleship.

THE CHARACTERISTICS OF A SHEPHERD-LEADER

When we talk about the shepherd-leader, we are talking about a disciple maker. When those of us who grew up in the church or some form of Christian subculture hear the word *discipleship*, we automatically picture the Dr. Pepper commercial: a grandfatherly figure is sitting on the front porch with a young man, dispensing nuggets of wisdom while they watch the sun rise and clink their bottles together. Some of us have been fortunate enough to experience this sort of relationship. For others, though, the concept of discipleship creates a picture in our minds of a gigantic box that is overwhelming and intimidating in size, but it doesn't have anything in it. We see discipleship as a lofty and unattainable talent on the upper end of the spiritual hierarchy, something that we will do someday when we are more mature.

Biblical discipleship is simply the exchange of truth in the context of authentic relationships. To quote Steve Timmis from his book *Total Church*, "Life is the context of discipleship and the Word of God is its content."[7]

> *And when he returned to Capernaum after some days, it was reported that he was at home. And many were gathered together, so that there was no more room, not even at the door. And he was preaching the word to them. And they came, bringing to him a paralytic carried by four men. And when they could not get near him because of the crowd, they removed the roof above him, and when they had made an opening,*

they let down the bed on which the paralytic lay. And
when Jesus saw their faith, he said to the paralytic,
"Son, your sins are forgiven." (Mark 2:1–5)

This story works as a great example for us as we talk
about discipleship in community. The call of God on our
lives is to go and make disciples. The qualification for that
call is a transformed life and authority rooted in Jesus. We
are to be active participants in the mission of God. Gospel
flow in group life begins then not with the curriculum or
catchy acronyms, but with a person whose life has been
transformed by the gospel of Jesus Christ and who is on
mission to see that reconciliation takes place in every sphere
of life. In short, disciples make disciples who make disciples.
When this becomes the grid for how we raise up group
leaders, it puts the primary mission of the church at the
forefront of your group life.

At The Village, we describe a shepherd-leader as someone
with the following characteristics:

1. A love for Jesus
2. A love for the Scriptures
3. A love for people
4. A calling to leadership

We define a person with *a love for Jesus* as someone who
has shown evidences of grace in their life and is actively

growing in the maturity of their faith. When we walk new candidates through our leadership pipeline, we want to know if they understand and can articulate the gospel, but we also want to see indications of their growth in Christ. This isn't where we separate the superheroes from the everyday Joes. It is, however, where we separate the good-intentioned from those who are actually pursuing a growing relationship with Christ. Our questions are going to center around their testimony and spiritual formation.

J. Oswald Sanders said, "We can lead others only as far along the road as we ourselves have traveled."[8] What we are looking for here is not someone who has reached a benchmark of spiritual growth, but someone whose trajectory is healthy and a path that we would feel comfortable having people journey along with them. God has wired each of us so distinctively! There is so much beauty in how God has created us each differently, and we want to celebrate the fact that one person's pursuit of Jesus might look different from another's. The key attribute for us to ascertain about the leader is "active pursuit." Do they understand the gospel? Do they understand grace and reconciliation? Do they understand the mission of God? How has the gospel changed their life?

Love for the Scriptures is defined as someone with confidence to communicate truth from the Word of God. We are not talking about Bible scholars or even Bible teachers. This is someone who is consistently seeking to bring his or her life under the rule of Christ. One great way we are able to measure this is to not only have them describe how they are growing in their knowledge and application of the Bible, but to present common life scenarios that they might be walking their people through and ask them how they would counsel a person in that situation from the Bible. We break down several scenarios and give them an opportunity to explain how they would pastor people in those situations. Just because someone is able to articulate a theology around the sovereignty of God doesn't mean they are able to put that into practice when a real-life situation happens. We look for potential leaders who know that the Word of God is living and active and able to handle our questions, concerns, and struggles when we turn to it for guidance.

A love for people is exhibited by a person longing to see others grow in the maturity of their faith. The common denominator of every small group is people. Leading a group means dealing in the messiness of resistance. There are going to be those who just cannot or will not repent of their junk and press into Jesus. There will be those who, like the paralytic in Mark 2, just aren't able to get there because they are crippled in their sin and struggle. A shepherd-leader's role is one of longsuffering. Heart change doesn't happen overnight. It might take place through a group study time; things might finally click on a mission trip to South Sudan; or it may even happen as someone goes about their daily routine, for example. A leader who has a love for people is not someone who simply knows the formula for change or who manipulates for change, but someone who out of love presses on and pursues their people past the walls they erect out of pride, embarrassment, or fear.

The final ingredient we look for is *leadership calling.* Leading a small group is not for everyone. There is a specific nature to the demands of this ministry. When challenging someone to consider group leadership, we always reiterate that we are not asking something extrabiblical of them. The role of a group leader is to make disciples, so before those twenty people show up in your living room, there needs to be prayerful consideration about the leader's calling and readiness to engage in a shepherding role at that level.

Now this list is by no means exhaustive. There are nuances to these questions and different ways to achieve the same result. We want to raise the bar of leadership to a healthy level. When the threshold of entry is high for leaders, their results are going to be higher. When the threshold of entry is lower, the output will also be lower. If we want to see our groups become communities of faith carrying out the mission of God, then we have to place a higher priority on what is being presented week in and week out in those groups. If you place someone as a leader whose walk with the Lord is minimal to nonexistent, but who really desires to serve, you will get a group that drowns in the deep end of struggle because their leader doesn't know how to swim. Is this grid foolproof? Absolutely not, but if Sanders is correct and we can only lead people as far as we ourselves have traveled, then we shouldn't be surprised when a low standard of leadership goes such a short distance.

THE FUNCTION OF A SHEPHERD-LEADER

At The Village we place a high premium on those we place in that living room week in and week out. Our spiritual-formation process is rooted in the vehicle of group life. This means that groups provide the primary avenue for care and mobilization of our people. The role of a shepherd-leader at The Village is one who:

- *Cares* for and counsels group members
- *Encourages* group members to maturity in faith through the understanding and application of Scripture
- *Models* Christ and the fullness of joy found in Him

- *Mobilizes* the group to serve the body an incarnate gospel through multiplication efforts locally and globally

As we talked about earlier in this chapter, the common denominator for all group life is people. There is a 100 percent chance that your leaders will deal in the messiness of sin with their members on week one. One of the tangible benefits to moving your congregation toward a model of small groups is that it allows you to build a network within your body to provide care and counsel. Whether you are a small church of 100, or a large church of 10,000, there is probably not enough pastoral staff to provide the oversight and care needed to faithfully shepherd the entire congregation. By empowering our leaders to care for the flock, we return the mission of God to the people of God, equipping the saints to do and be what God has called them to do and be. Providing pastoral *care* in group life means having an environment that is:

- *Genuine and Authentic*—A place that consistently works to tear down the walls that we erect out of pride, embarrassment, fear, isolation, individualism and sin
- *Safe*—A place to confess struggles, sins, and doubts and to share our sufferings and joys

- *Intentional*—A place to work together by applying God's Word, pushing back darkness, helping the poor, reaching the lost, and loving one another

Our role as pastors is to equip and guide our people to be the Church to one another. From discipline to benevolence, through equipping our leaders to shepherd well, we make ministry the responsibility of the whole body of Christ. There is no substitute for the body being the body! We purposefully use the word *encourage* instead of *teach* because we believe that applying God's Word involves more than teaching and that not every group leader needs to have the gift of teaching in order to faithfully lead their group through the study and application of the Scriptures.

We will discuss "alignment" in chapter 5, but providing structure to your groups in terms of what they study and how they spend their time is key. At The Village we create sermon studies for our small groups, to go along with the preaching series. These studies don't hinge on what is taught weekly, but rather seek to complement the study that week. They are text based, which means if the sermon comes from Matthew 5, then our hope is that by the combination of attending service and going through the group's material, one would have a comprehensive study of that particular text. This could play out a number of ways in your church;

at The Village, we desire to connect the stage to the living room.

Our people spend a good amount of time every week listening to dynamic and faithful teaching, so our sermon studies free our group leaders up from trying to create a didactic model and allow them to dive deep into the waters of application. As we have mentioned before, we don't require group leaders to be the spiritually elite; we do, however, expect them to be someone whose spiritual trajectory is one of progressive sanctification. The group has to play as crucial a role in the leader's life as it does the other group members because we don't graduate from the gospel. We need people consistently working to tear down the walls of isolationism in our lives.

A shepherd-leader is one who *models* a pursuit of Christ. We are constantly asking this question about our groups' leaders: Would we be comfortable having someone imitate their walk with Jesus? If the answer is no, then you probably have someone leading your group who is either stagnant and needs to repent, doesn't know Jesus and needs to repent, or who is immature and doesn't know what it means to follow Christ and needs a leader who does.

So, every healthy tree bears good fruit, but the dis-eased tree bears bad fruit. A healthy tree cannot bear

bad fruit, nor can a diseased tree bear good fruit.
(Matt. 7:17–18)

Would you feel comfortable having the people in your church learn the pursuit of Christ by modeling their lives after your leaders? If the answer is no, then you have to look at your filter for raising up and establishing group leaders. Do you want your groups to be spiritually healthy? Raising the bar of who you allow to lead groups in your church will have an exponential impact not only on the depth of your group life, but also on your leadership development. Good leaders beget good leaders. Bad leaders beget bad leaders.

The last expectation that should be placed on your leaders is mobilization for mission. The temptation for groups is the same as the temptation for us as individuals, to be inwardly focused. As Tim Chester says, "Sin is fundamentally an orientation toward self."[9] Groups are a great place for sin to be confessed and warred against, God's Word to be studied and applied, and needs to be prayed for and met. Yet, this cannot be where the flow of the gospel stops in your community. A gospel that terminates on you and me is not the gospel. We have been saved both *from* something and *for* something. Discipleship in your groups will hit a frustrating low ceiling when the gospel does not flow out of the groups and into the spheres of influence around them.

Mission can take a number of different forms in group life. We say often that one of the biggest ways our groups can be missional (oriented toward mission) is to plant new groups throughout our city. The more geographically based communities we have living the gospel in their everyday lives, the better chance we have of reaching our city for Jesus. Gospel multiplication is multifaceted and we need to be encouraging this to be contextual in the lives of our communities.

I recently met with a couple that leads a group not far from our largest campus. This group has been meeting for about a year and a half, so I was pressing them on how the gospel is flowing in and out of their group. When I asked if they were ready to plant a new group, they said no. I was surprised and disappointed to hear this so I started to inquire about what was going on in their group. What they said next blew me out of the water! They began telling me about all God was doing, how they as leaders felt conviction to pursue adoption and within a year a child was placed with them. The whole home group showed up to the couple's house on the day they received their child and as a community welcomed that baby into the family. Soon after, another family in the group was convicted in the same way and within months God answered their prayers and they received a child. As if this wasn't enough, the leaders started talking about another couple in their group who were burdened for the lost people in Japan and are now moving there to be full-time missionaries and the entire group is supporting them.

If my only standard for measuring this group's health was whether they were starting new groups, I would have missed it. Gospel multiplication can play out a number of ways in any given context, with beautiful diversity. The movement is going to start somewhere. Be very intentional about who you place in leadership, and pour into them deeply. The gospel fruit you will reap from this investment will be well worth the effort.

When we put a low bar of expectations on those we place in leadership over our people, the fruit from their work mirrors the expectations. Who you give responsibility of spiritual leadership in that living room and the clarity you provide for direction will heavily impact the depth of your group life. Below are some questions to help you examine where you are in the process of building toward gospel-centered community.

DISCUSSION QUESTIONS

1. What are the primary goals of your group life? Discipleship? Connection?

2. What are the expectations of your leadership? Shepherding? Facilitating? Hosting?

3. What hurdles or ceilings are you hitting in your group ministry?

4. What steps do you need to take to begin moving toward health?

CHAPTER 2

COMMUNITY CORRUPTED

Recovering community starts by recovering a complete, correct view of both God and humanity. So we begin at the beginning. The creation account in Genesis 1–2 sets in motion the way we are to relate to one another. Genesis 1:26–27 tells us God purposefully created men and women in His own image. Think about this for a second: a triune being created a single being to reflect the image of a triune being. Seems a little bizarre doesn't it? Even the greatest theologians find this one perplexing. A. W. Tozer, reflecting on what we call the "Trinity," said, "Our sincerest effort to grasp the incomprehensible mystery of the Trinity must remain forever futile, and only by deepest reverence can it be saved from actual presumption."[1] In other words, we will never fully understand the Trinity, and we may be in trouble when we think we do. Yet God chose to reveal Himself this way, and He also chose to design us to reflect that image.

Now why does that matter beyond the seminary classroom? It means God has hardwired us to go to Him to learn about ourselves. Here's the point: the deeper we dive into the nature of God, the more we learn about the nature of man. This is where we must begin our recovery of community.

The Trinity is our model for community. We will never perfectly replicate it because we are both finite and sinful. God knew we would be that way when He created us, yet He created us in His image anyway. In fact, God, when looking on man after creation, in Genesis 2 describes his existence as incomplete. Stop and soak in this scene: God looks at man and says this will not do, you shouldn't be alone. This is before sin ever enters the picture! Community was not God's response to sin but a building block in the DNA of our creational image. So our imperfection does not stop us from looking to the perfect godhead to learn who we are and how we are to live because the image of God wasn't destroyed in the fall, but distorted. If God is the perfect community, then building a community that reflects Him is our responsibility to the people He's placed around us. This is why Bruce Ware said, "We can be confident that when we live out what God is like we will enter into the good that he has designed for us to know."[2]

Let's look at what the Bible tells us about the Trinity and the implications for Christian community. We'll look at one truth, then examine its implications for our practice before moving on to the next one.

Truth: We are created by God for community.

> *Then God said, "Let us make man in our image, after* ***our*** *likeness. And let* ***them*** *have dominion over the fish of the sea and over the birds of the heavens and over the livestock and over all the earth and over every creeping thing that creeps on the earth." So God created man in his own image, in the image of God he created him; male and female he created* ***them***. (Gen. 1:26–27, emphasis added)

Orthodox Christian teaching says the God of the Bible is one essence and three distinct persons: God the Father, God the Son, and God the Holy Spirit. These three persons coexist in perfect harmony in eternity. The Westminster Confession of Faith, one of the most well-known doctrinal statements in church history, sums up the nature of God this way: "In the unity of the Godhead there are three persons, of one substance, power, and eternity: God the Father, God the Son, and God the Holy Spirit."[3]

According to the Scripture passage above, we are created in the image of the Trinity. This simple idea carries massive implications, only one of which we will explore in depth. This reality separates Christianity from every other religion. We are not merely subjects of God (Islam), we are not trying to attain godhood (Mormonism), and we are not a part of God (eastern mysticism). We are in the *likeness* of God. We reflect Him. Philip Ryken and Michael LeFebvre say it this way:

> From all eternity, the three Persons have enjoyed perfect love within the Godhead. When it pleased God to make mankind in his own image, he created us as social beings. We were created for relationship with God and to reflect his likeness not merely as individuals but in relationship with one another. This may be why the author of Genesis dared to use plural pronouns to describe God at that point in the creation account where he tells of God's creating mankind in his own likeness . . . God made man a social being because the prototype for man—God himself—is a being in communion.[4]

This is why the community of Christians carries such influencing power in its surrounding context. When rightly practiced, Christians doing life together literally put God on display. And when they do, Jesus said the world will come to know Him through it. If you are a Christian, do not let the familiarity of this knowledge diminish its power for you. The creator and sustainer of the universe, the great "I Am," has decided that YOU are going to be His representation on the earth. The implications of this truth stretch far beyond the limits of our ability to explain.

Did you catch God employing plural pronouns *(we)* in the creation account? Mankind is the only created being God described creating in community. Because He is relational we are—by design—relational creatures. The very next chapter (Gen. 2) reinforces this communal image.

> *Then the Lord God said, "It is not good that the man should be alone; I will make him a helper fit for him."* (Gen. 2:18)

The very first thing "not good" in the Bible was Adam's solitude. How could God make something "not good"? As the story progresses, we see that man alone wasn't "bad," he was just incomplete. In other words, God wasn't finished yet. So God created a companion for man in the form of woman. Man was an incomplete image of God alone. Alone he could not depend on another, nor help another. Alone, he had no one like him to love or to be loved by. Alone, he was missing out on something God clearly wanted for him. After God created Eve, they were "very good." Do you see the imprint of God's nature all over this? Bruce Ware's reflection is helpful here.

> "The very fact that God, though singular in nature, is plural and societal in person, indicates that we should not view ourselves as isolated individuals who happen to exist in close proximity to others, but as interconnected, interdependent relational persons in community. It is not enough just to exist together alongside but independent of others, along the lines of how a lot of guys live in a dorm—sharing space with other guys whom they just pass in the hall. They exist in close proximity, but is there really a relationship of community in many such cases? God intends that there be a created community of persons in which there is an interconnection and interdependence, so that what one does affects the other, what one needs can be supplied by the other, and what one seeks to accomplish can be assisted by the other."[5]

The more Adam and Eve's lives became interdependently connected, the more they were "very good" in God's eyes: relational unity, yet distinct in roles and personality. The beautiful image of God reflected in humanity was people living interdependently in the place God had designed, according to the way God had instructed. This is community. The people God created leveraging the gifts He gave them to live for the benefit of one another and others according to His design.

Implication: Community is not a church program.

We can only live out God's purpose for us to reflect His image when we live in community. This creational mandate must influence the way we perceive community in our local churches. In light of the created image, it's not just unfortunate if there are people in your church who aren't in some kind of God-reflecting community, it is unbiblical and subhuman. To that end, if you or your church is content with merely making community a program people can participate in (small groups, Sunday school, missional communities, etc.), we want to challenge you to reconsider your approach. We aren't talking here about enhancing the impressive rhetoric your announcement guy uses on the weekend to talk about your community programs. We are talking about letting your theology drive your methodology. The Scriptures have several metaphors we will unpack later to help describe how the people of God are to relate to one another.[6]

Let us be clear up front: we are not opposed to building programs to support gospel community in your church. In fact, churches would be foolish not to facilitate community in their church with intentional support. But if that is all we are doing, if we believe we can then check "community" off our to-do list, we have missed the point entirely. Community cannot be outsourced, no matter how sophisticated the strategy. Gospel community must become a part of every church member's personal lifestyle in order to connect God's people with the people of God, because community is something that is lived out, not attended.

Of all of the metaphors the Bible uses to describe God's people relating to one another, it never once calls the church an audience. Let's pause here for a second. The time, energy, and resources you devote to how you "do church" stem directly out of your theology. Belief always drives practice.

We have two ways of thinking about this implication that have been very convicting and challenging to us. The following two questions aren't intended as an attack, but might be conversation starters for the leadership of your church. I (Spence) will share with you how our leadership at the Summit Church walked through these two questions.

1. *Where does community stack up in your priorities?* Here's the thing. We always knew we wanted to be about "disciple making," not "audience growing." That wasn't a sudden lightbulb that went off. With that said, we realized we were not structuring ourselves to reflect our values.

While we said we valued community, we were not doing much to demonstrate it. And a value is worthless if that is all it is. What you do displays what you believe. So we had to rethink what we were doing to line it up with what we said we believed.

So we simplified and reorganized our community strategy. For us, that meant small groups became the hub for discipleship in our church. We decided elders would coach small-group leaders, we committed to building a small-groups staff team, and we even canceled some regular church events in order to give groups priority on our families' weekly calendar. Our budget was adjusted to reflect these changes. Pastoral care through community became a priority reflected in our bottom line. This moved us from just talking about community to buying in to the idea. I reject the notion that what happens on the weekend is more important than the weekday; I believe treating it like that is looking at both worship gatherings and small groups as church *programs*, when we should be seeing them both as functions of one, whole biblical community. We will talk about this in our chapter on alignment, but as a teaser the weekend and the week should work together.

2. How do you communicate community? Once we decided community was a priority, we had to figure out how to communicate the idea well. We had to get beyond talking about small groups as a program to connect people, and get to community as the *imago dei*. Small groups are merely a starting point for our people to begin living out this priority in the life of our church.

First, our lead pastor asked me to sit in on his weekly sermon-planning meeting. As he walked through the sermon he was going to preach the coming weekend, I looked for places to communicate the theology and practice of community. It meant we preached a few sermons devoted to unpacking the theology of community. It meant we led by sharing our own stories of how God was changing us into His image through community. In doing so, we were making the abstract idea of community more accessible.

Second, we began collecting stories that illustrated gospel community. We found groups (both formal and informal groups) where people were serving one another, caring for one another, and intentionally encouraging one another in their obedience to God. For example, the church heard about Drew's small group, which collected over $1500 to pay for a surgery a guy at his gym needed, and how he came to faith through the love of group members.

Community needs to be more than doctrine. The doctrine of community is like the framework of a house. The stories shared are the windows and paint that draws you to it. Now we are hearing story after story of how God has changed lives through small groups across our church.

Truth: The Trinity is three interdependent persons in community.

The longer I'm part of a church staff, the more I learn about something I never knew anything about. I always loved music, but until recently I didn't know much about how it worked. Thankfully, our worship leaders graciously answer all my annoying questions.

Jonathan Welch and Matt Papa, two of our worship pastors, indulged me as I was researching for this chapter. Music is built on chords, and chords are built on triads. A triad is three notes spaced at precise intervals to create a harmonious sound. I love going into our worship gathering ahead of time and watching the musicians transform from a bunch of individuals holding instruments to one band creating one textured, awesome sound. In that moment, they move beyond unity to harmony. If they all held the same instruments and played the exact same notes, they would have unity, right? But none of us would be overly impressed. But when they all play different instruments with different notes that all blend together into one harmony, it's awesome. They are unique individuals with unique roles and responsibilities that are all interdependently working together to create one harmonious sound.

While all metaphors, this one included, will fall short of explaining the nature of God, this is one of the better metaphors for understanding how the Trinity works together. The three persons in the Trinity have distinctly different roles yet are one in the same being. Just like the notes of a triad, the three persons of the Trinity carry out specific roles yet function as one harmonious being. They are neither codependent nor independent, but interdependent persons living and functioning eternally together in peace and harmony. They do not duplicate one another, but complement one another in the way they interact with one another and with the world.

Implication: The power of God is displayed through community.

One of my favorite authors is C. S. Lewis. In his book *Mere Christianity* he said:

"God can show Himself as He really is only to real men. And that means not simply to men who are individually good, but to men who are united together in a body, loving one another, helping one another, showing Him to one another. For that is what God meant humanity to be like; like players in one band, or organs in one body.

Consequently, the one really adequate instrument for learning about God is the whole Christian community, waiting for Him together."[7]

Lewis had been part of a group of three friends for a long time when one of them passed away. Initially he tried to console himself by telling himself he would get to know his remaining friend better, because he would no longer have to share him.

I believe this is comparable to what Lewis is saying about our knowledge of God in the absence of participating in authentic Christian community. There are aspects of God's grace, power, wisdom, and holiness that I will never draw out in my limited life span and experience.

But Lewis found that there was a side of his living friend that was only brought out by his deceased friend. Even the increase of time and attention allowed by heightened exclusivity of their friendship could not generate the same *kind* of knowing.

When I immerse myself in the lives of others whose life stories reflect distinct aspects of God's grace, power, wisdom, and holiness, I come to know more of God. God does not change, but I know more of Him than I could have comprehended in isolation.

For you and me today this means there is hope for our relationships. If God designed us for relationships, then there must be something in relationship that far exceeds life in isolation. It means community is worth fighting for!

It means marriages are meant to be healthy, enriching relationships that reflect the love of God for us. It means parenting is to be a love-filled relationship reflecting the care of the Father for us. It means work is to be an act of worship to the God whose work created us. Instead of looking out for No. 1, we are to mutually trust one another, and work together in reflection of the triune God. I don't know about you, but I want these kinds of relationships. We'll see in a little bit why we don't always get them like we want, but there is still hope for them when we seek to display the image of God with one another. There is hope for our world when they see that image on display among us, which brings us to a third truth.

Truth: Sin distorts the image of God in our community.

Anyone who has been in a relationship, of any kind, for more than about two weeks will tell you "relationships are messy." They are full of conflict, uncertainty, ambiguity, and misunderstandings. Two people in a dating relationship have different ideas of how far along they are. Two coworkers disagree on methods for customer acquisition, two friends each begin to wonder if the other is drifting away. And those are the tame examples, right? *Adultery, abuse, neglect, betrayal, sabotage, attack, revenge, abandonment* are all words given to actions taken by one person toward another person. Messy. Encouraged yet? Let's keep going.

The same thing is true for community. Community is messy, maybe messier than single relationships. A community isn't just one relationship, but a web of interwoven relationships. So if one relationship can be messy to maintain, just imagine the mess a community can be! Let's briefly look at *why* that is, and what can be done about it.

In Genesis, the Bible records the moment often referred to as the fall of man. Adam and Eve were perfectly reflecting the communal image they were created in. They existed interdependently together in the garden just as God had designed. In Genesis 2, God tells Adam not to eat of the tree of the knowledge of good and evil. Next chapter, Genesis 3, Eve decides to disobey God and eats the fruit. Then she gives it to Adam, and he eats. What happened in that moment altered the world forever. It was right there that sin (choosing self over God) entered the world and separated man from a sinless God. And the curse of sin followed. God said man would no longer have a peaceful life but a hard life. Work would be hard. For the woman, childbearing would be painful. And their lives would now have an end—death. In Romans 5:12 Paul gives us a divinely inspired explanation of the significance of this event:

> "Therefore just as sin came into the world through one man, and death through sin, and so death spread to all men because all sinned."

Basically, in this moment, the world was broken. Sin created a permanent scar on creation, which spread to every person ever born. So now the world isn't as it should be. This may be the most agreeable tenet in all of Christianity to those outside the faith. Every day we see evidence of the world not being as it should. I'm sure you can give examples in both the news and in your personal life showing how messed up life can be.

Implication: Building community is hard work.

Any marriage-enrichment message worth hearing or reading will say something like "marriage is hard work." Marriage, like every other relationship, is hard work because it is a relationship between two sinful people. I watched an interview of a high-profile Christian leader and his wife shortly after news broke of this leader's adultery. The interviewer asked the wife how she was able to stay with this guy after such betrayal. Her response, permanently etched in my brain, was, "We have to stop being surprised when people sin." That's a game changer. She wasn't saying we shouldn't trust people, she was simply acknowledging we are sinners living in imperfect relationships with one another. We'll come back to this in the next chapter, but what she acknowledged here is that even marriage is not immune to the effects of sin.

Building a community that reflects the love and unity of God is just as, if not more, difficult than building a healthy marriage. If you are in any way responsible for building and maintaining community in your setting, understanding this principle is critical to your survival. I've seen many small-group leaders burn out because the group of twelve they are doing group life with falls far short of the community they had dreamed up in their heads when they decided to lead a group. I find Dietrich Bonhoeffer's words on this very helpful.

> "Every human wish dream that is injected into the Christian community is a hindrance to genuine community and must be banished if genuine community is to survive. . . . God hates visionary dreaming; it makes the dreamer proud and pretentious. The man who fashions a visionary ideal of community demands that it be realized by God, by others, and by himself. He enters the community of Christians with

his demands, sets his own law, and judges the brethren and God Himself accordingly . . . We enter into
that common life not as demanders but as thankful
recipients."[8]

There is probably nothing more important for me to hear
and heed as a pastor responsible for building community in
my local church. I love "vision casting." I love giving my
people something to dream for. But dreams that leave out
the reality of sin are dangerous and shallow. Including the
reality of sin and its impact on community does two things
for you and those you lead.

First, it creates realistic expectations for the group
in regards to what their experience will be. Instead of a
utopian dreamworld the members of your group will have
a ready awareness that everyone coming in has a history, a
personality, and a propensity to sin in some way or another.

Second, it greatly heightens the need for active grace
among the members of the community. Without sin there is
no need for grace. Only sinners need grace. So when I train
small-group leaders at our church, I do everything I can to
make it clear they will have ample opportunity to practice
grace with those in their group. That is, they will have plenty
of chances to love as Christ loves in response to the sins of
their group members. Only a community that understands it

is going to sin can be a community that readily and actively practices grace with one another.

Truth: Biblical community is the final apologetic.

"A new commandment I give to you, that you love one another: just as I have loved you, you also are to love one another. By this all people will know that you are my disciples, if you have love for one another." (John 13:34–35)

Francis Schaeffer was one of the most influential Christian minds in the twentieth century. One of his central theses was that the way Christians interacted with one another would be the final apologetic for whether or not non-Christians believed the gospel message. In his book *The Mark of a Christian* he reflected on that idea.

"Yet, without true Christians loving one another, Christ says the world cannot be expected to listen, even when we give proper answers. Let us be careful, indeed, to spend a lifetime studying to give honest answers. For years the orthodox, evangelical church has done this very poorly. So it is well to spend time learning to answer the questions of men who are about us. But after we have done our best to communicate to a lost world, still we must never forget that the final apologetic which Jesus gives is the observable love of true Christians for true Christians."[9]

Chapters 13 through 17 of the Gospel of John hold some of the richest words in Scripture, especially as they relate to our understanding of community. In John 13, as Schaeffer observed, Jesus is saying something very profound about Christian community. God has designed community to be a litmus test to the validity of the gospel message to the watching world. Jesus goes on to pray in John 17:20–23:

> I do not ask for these only, but also for those who will believe in me through their word, that they may all be one, just as you, Father, are in me, and I in you, that they also may be in us, so that the world may believe that you have sent me. The glory that you have given me I have given to them, that they may be one even as we are one, I in them and you in me, that they may become perfectly one, so that the world may know that you sent me and loved them even as you loved me.

Can you hear the memory of creation in Jesus' prayer? Jesus is asking for Christians to have the same level of unity that exists in the Trinity. He is praying for God to mold them into their created image! And He is asking this for a purpose.

Unity among Christians is paramount because this is how the watching world will know of God's love for it. Christian unity is the litmus test for the Christian message.

Implication: Community must be accessible.

The visibility of the Christian community among non-Christians will be discussed in chapter 7, but we should acknowledge some initial implications of our theology here.

If the Christian community serving one another in love and grace is a powerful argument for the truth of Christ's message, then we must ensure this community is accessible to non-Christians, right? At this point you may be asking if we are about to drift into a dialogue about the pros and cons of open versus closed small groups. No way. That's a side issue based on the model you chose. The theological implication is simply that your community of Christians must be accessible to non-Christians somehow.

I was with a church planter in Boston, Massachusetts, recently who was sharing with me how he goes about building a congregation. When I asked him about things like inviter cards, mail-outs, and Web promo ads, he smiled at me and said something I will never forget: "Bus ads with my face on it." I'm kidding; he didn't say that. That's ridiculous (but I got your attention, didn't I?). He pointed to the guy at the table next to us in the coffee shop and said, "It would be less offensive for me, right now, to go invite that guy to a strip club than it would be to invite him to a church worship service." Whoa—and I'm pretty sure next-table-over-guy heard him too. He proceeded to tell me that the front doors to his church are accessed through small pockets of their congregation living in community with one another and inviting non-Christians they know into their community.

That church planter is not alone. Interest in attending worship gatherings has faded in many areas, but spiritual interest isn't going anywhere. Three out of five young, unchurched people say "they would be willing to study the Bible if a friend asked them to do so."[10] People still want to engage truth; they just want to see it on display as well. We need to go beyond sitting side by side in worship services; we have to be extremely intentional to practice Christian community in a way that is accessible to non-Christians.[11] Again, we will hit more on the *how* later in the book.

CONCLUSION

Our practice of community must be drawn intentionally from our understanding of who God is. What better starting point could there be for us as the Church? After all, leading people into the presence of God as the foundation for their life as a Christian should be among our top priorities.

In summary, here are the four truths related to the image of God and their implications for our lives:

Truth	Implication
We are created by God for community.	Community is not a church program.
The Trinity is three inter-dependent persons in community.	The power of God is displayed through community.
Sin distorts the image of God in our community.	Building community is hard work.
Biblical community is the final apologetic.	Community must be accessible.

In the Trinity we have a road map, a guide for how we are to live with one another.

DISCUSSION QUESTIONS

1. What connections do you see between the Trinity and community?

2. How can a better understanding of the Trinity improve your understanding of community?

3. What role does sin play in community?

CHAPTER 3

THE DISTINCTIVES OF A GOSPEL COMMUNITY

"Jesus is not just the basis for Christian community, but the means of it."
DIETRICH BONHOEFFER

Every community is built on something that binds you together. I'm fascinated by the niche subcultures that will form around the most bizarre things. Did you know there is a small group of people who've given the focus of their lives to competing over the original arcade version of Donkey Kong? Groups form around seemingly random things because people, whether they believe it or not, are hardwired for community. When people give themselves to a like-minded community, we see their blueprint coming out. They long for acceptance, love, and security. And while God designed people to express those longings, He intends for

Christ to satisfy them. Until that one thing we give ourselves to is Jesus, we experience false, disappointing versions of the true community we are created for.

#PASTORFAIL

As the small-groups pastor of my church, I (Spence) once believed that my group was supposed to be the very best one in our local body. But God taught me, at the age of twenty-seven, a costly lesson in humility. Thankfully, He also showed me the power of the gospel when put at the front and center of real life.

At the time, we "stacked the deck" in our small group, with two other pastors from the church, along with their wives. Josh and Dave (not their real names) in particular were two of my closest friends, so to work and play together was rewarding for all of us. Courtney and I loved that group of people, and I still look back on it as one of the richest seasons of fellowship that I've had.

But that all came screeching to a halt one night while Josh and I were driving to an indoor soccer game. Josh began describing to me a situation at the church that was beginning to get out of control. A work relationship with one of his staff members had turned into a deep emotional relationship. Work hours had become relationship hours, and they were clocking those hours at a fast pace. The relationship was later given the label "emotional affair" because while no physical intimacy ever occurred, an inappropriate bond had nonetheless been cultivated between Josh and this woman, Lisa (that's what we'll call her), Dave's wife.

You read that correctly; there was an emotional affair with two married people who were members of our group. So much for the dream-team small group, right? An affair between a pastor and another pastor's wife developed right under the nose of the small-groups pastor. The following days were filled with tears and pain as Josh and Lisa both went through the confession and repentance process with their spouses, our church staff, and our church. We wept with Dave and with Josh's wife, Andrea, as they dealt with the pain of betrayal. In the months to come, both families had to endure the pain of any mistakes our pastoral team made as they tried to guide the restoration process. Needless to say, it was a mess.

In those moments, we experienced the *power* of the gospel in ways we hadn't before. I watched the people of God surround both of these marriages and rehearse the gospel minute by minute, hour by hour, day by day.

Lisa heard the absolution of Romans 8:1—that "there is . . . now no condemnation for those who are in Christ Jesus." With the help of a counselor, friends, and (most notably) Dave, Lisa uncovered and dealt with many issues from her past during this season.

Josh heard the *freedom* of the gospel, which brought him strength in a time of true brokenness and failure. 1 John 1:9 says, "If we confess our sins, he is faithful and just to forgive us . . . from all unrighteousness."

Both Dave and Andrea heard the *humility* of the gospel which empowered Dave to fight for Lisa even while she was still running from him and motivated Andrea to forgive her husband and find healing in their marriage. Philippians 2:8 says of Christ that "being found in human form, he humbled himself by becoming obedient to the point of death, even death on a cross."

*The only thing strong enough to build and sustain Christian community is the gospel **and the refuge found therein.*** Demographics, money, location, shared interests, curriculum, or good causes will not create the deep, true community for which God designed us. In many respects those things will only serve to disappoint and even destroy, if they are the basis for the community.

The Bible talks about this new community formed by and lived through the gospel. As we look into it, what you need to hear is that such a community is indeed possible. It isn't a perfect community; we established that in the previous chapter and saw it afresh with Dave, Lisa, Josh, and Andrea. We must not think about "true community" in terms of perfection, but in terms of reflection. That means doing our best to reflect the community of the Trinity as we live together, knowing our sin will both cause us to fall short and allow us to give and receive grace. While the Bible uses several metaphors for this new community, three stand out: Scripture calls the Church a new people, a new family, and a new body. Each metaphor highlights distinctives of who we are as a gospel community.

A NEW PEOPLE

Our oldest son, Zeke, was born on August 8, 2008. I know: 8.8.08 makes it pretty easy on us to remember! He was born literally 30 minutes before the start of the opening ceremonies of the 2008 Summer Olympics in Beijing. So my wife and I sat there in the hospital room as brand-new parents, hanging out with our little boy, watching the opening ceremonies. I sat there with him and introduced him to the world as each team proudly waved their country's flag while being introduced during the traditional parade of nations that happens at every opening ceremony.

There in the opening ceremonies, each nation's representatives are dressed in clothing designed to reflect something distinct about their country. These athletes show great pride as they represent their countries to the entire world on that night. The host country also gets the chance to put on an opening show that introduces the world to their heritage and culture. Anyone who saw the '08 opening ceremonies will easily recall the vivid imagery on display as the world was introduced to the China of yesterday, today, and tomorrow.

The opening ceremonies of the Olympics remind the world that it is not just an alphabetical drop-down list of countries with different names. Each nation has cultural distinctives like language, shared history, and traditions that set them apart from other nations. In the opening ceremonies, we get just a little taste of these from around the world.

The Bible uses the wording "new people" to describe the people of God. First Peter 2:9–10 says:

But you are a chosen race, a royal priesthood, a holy nation, a people for his own possession, that you may proclaim the excellencies of him who called you out of darkness into his marvelous light. Once you were not a people, but now you are God's people; once you had not received mercy, but now you have received mercy.

If you read all of 1 Peter 2, you will find that the Christian community is given many descriptions, but this idea of a new people—God's people—stands out. It drives home an idea that I don't think many in America understand. Salvation was intended for a group, not an individual. The Bible primarily teaches that Christ died for a people, not a person. Now, you can't have a "people" without persons, so I am not discounting the individual act of repentance and faith that comes in response to hearing and believing the gospel. The Holy Spirit indeed saves you personally, but the Scriptures seem to focus on the salvation and creation of a new people.

When you become a Christian, you become a part of the people Christ came to rescue. It's impossible to divorce a Christian from community, for to be Christian is to be part of a new people. It would be like one proudly wearing the American flag, reciting the Pledge of Allegiance daily, and then despising the United States. It wouldn't make sense, and we would say that person is a liar or an imposter. Likewise, you cannot separate your Christianity from the new community that you are born into when you believe the gospel. And just like a nation has cultural distinctives, so this new people has distinctives we call gospel distinctives— things the watching world should notice about the people of God. Here are two examples:

Gospel Distinctive: Grace

When the watching world observes the people of God, grace should be easy to spot. Peter reminds us that we previously had not received mercy, but now have received mercy. This mercy is the mercy shown by God to give salvation to us—who did not deserve it. Our heritage, what binds us together, is what has been done for us. The gospel message is that God sent Jesus to die the death we deserved for our sin so that we could be reconciled to Him. We say around our church all the time, the gospel in four words is "Jesus in my place." This is our heritage, our unifying ground as a people. If we are God's holy nation, the gospel is our founding declaration of freedom. It stands to reason we would be identified by this kind of grace in our interactions with one another. If our heritage is grace, so should our practice be.

Is your personal interaction with other Christians marked by grace? Are you quick to forgive people when they deliberately sin against you? Are you quick to show love to people who don't ask for it? The apostle John said this is how the world will recognize Christians: That "just as I have loved you, you also are to love one another. By this all people will know that you are my disciples, if you have love for one another" (John 13:34–35). Grace that reflects God's grace to us is a distinctive of the Church. So, how dominant is grace in your interactions with others? Are you known by it?

Gospel Distinctive: Sacrificial Generosity

Christians give generously of their time, resources, and energy as an act of thanksgiving for all God has given us. Our generosity does not flow from legalistic obligations, guilt, or fear. Rather, it flows from the life-altering realization that God was exceedingly generous with us by sending His Son to die for us. This means we practice the generosity we see in Acts 2:42–47. We actively look for ways to be generous, cultivating a spirit of generosity within ourselves. We look for opportunities to give to one another as any has need.

Is your life marked by generosity? Not just giving of your extra, but giving in such a way that it costs you something. Our salvation cost God His only Son, yet His love for His people compelled Him to do it. And so the people of God give joyfully to one another as they have need. What does your money say about your generosity? As a recovering penny-pincher, I can tell you the charitable contributions line on my tax return is painfully revealing for where my priorities were the past year. But please don't hear this as just a money question. What you do with your stuff is like a sign pointing to what you value. I long to hear, "Look at the way they keep giving their stuff to everyone who needs it. They must be Christians." When other people look at the people of God, our generosity should be plainly observed as a mark of who we are.

A NEW FAMILY

Matthew, Mark, and Luke all tell a story where Jesus is hanging out with His disciples, when a man runs in to tell Him His mom and brothers are outside and want to talk with Him. Jesus responds unexpectedly. He looks at this guy and says, "Who is my mother and who are my brothers?" Jesus sets us up for something revolutionary.

With His hand stretched out pointing back to the guys sitting around Him, He says, "Here are my mother and my brothers! For whoever does the will of my Father in heaven is my brother and sister and mother."[1] Jesus doesn't diminish the importance of the biological family; He merely elevates the importance of the spiritual family. In a sense, He reorders family lines around His blood. A new family was being established, one to endure throughout all generations for all time and into eternity. Now just as a Christian would be a citizen of two kingdoms, he would be a child in two families. And just as God's kingdom takes preeminence over the kingdom of earth, so God's family takes preeminence over the family on the earth. This was, and still is, revolutionary. Jesus reinforces the idea in Mark 10:29–30:

> *Truly, I say to you, there is no one who has left house or brothers or sisters or mother or father or children or lands, for my sake and for the gospel, who will not receive a hundredfold now in this time, houses and brothers and sisters and mothers and children and lands, with persecutions, and in the age to come eternal life.*

See that little word *now* in verse 30? It's significant. Do you know what it means? It means now! How do we receive a hundred times the houses and siblings and mothers and children? Where will they come from? The answer is the new family. Jesus is talking about the Church. In the Church, we find an extended family designed by God to be a redeemed and permanent version of the biological family. You may be thinking, "But I love my family. Are you saying I have to leave it?" No. John Piper once said it this way: "You must renounce the primacy of your natural relationships and follow Jesus into the fellowship of the family of God."[2]

Even marriage is less permanent than this new family. Jesus tells us that "in the resurrection they neither marry nor are given in marriage, but are like angels in heaven"

(Matt. 22:30). My wife and I used to be pretty depressed about that. Really, God? You aren't going to let us be married up there? Isn't that going to be a little awkward when we bump into each other? Am I going to put the moves on her again or punch another citizen of heaven when he eyeballs my now former wife? Well, the reality is that whatever does await us is better than marriage. Marriage is a sign designed to give us a glimpse into eternal life with Christ. So, while my relationship to my wife is temporary, my relationship to her as my sister in Christ is eternal. If I really believe that, it drastically alters the way I treat her in marriage. The primacy of our new family over our earthly one impacts how we communicate, how we spend our time, and how we care for one another. Now, we don't neglect one another as husband and wife. The Bible is clear that our marriage relationship has certain demands and expectations. But a new richness is brought to that marriage when I realize I am in this marriage with a daughter of God, a sister who I am called in this world to give the utmost attention and care to love, encourage, and protect. In the new family, our marriage and family relationships are secondary to our relationships as brothers and sisters in Christ. With that in mind, let's consider some of the distinctives we have as the family of God.

Gospel Distinctive: Diversity

I get the chance to teach our middle- and high-school students on occasion. If you know anything about that age range, visual aids and audience participation are important if you want to keep their attention. So I give everyone a name tag and have them write their first name and then the name Jesus in place of their last name. It's a little cheesy for sure. I get them to reintroduce themselves to one another as Spence Jesus, Pritesh Jesus, etc. The idea is that, in Christ, we all have new last names. Regardless of our race, social cliques, affluence, or athletic ability, we all wear the last name Jesus. We are the family that an onlooker would need an explanation to explain how we are, in fact, a family. The apostle Paul speaks of how our new family looks different than our biological family:

> "For in Christ Jesus you are all sons of God, through faith. For as many of you as were baptized into Christ have put on Christ. There is neither Jew nor Greek, there is neither slave nor free, there is no male and female, for you are all one in Christ Jesus. And if you are Christ's, then you are Abraham's offspring, heirs according to promise." (Gal. 3:26–29)

Our diversity is one of the most powerful distinctives that God has given His Church. Not just racial diversity, but also age and socioeconomic diversity are important for the family of God to celebrate. Think about Paul's words. Jews and Greeks hanging out together would be more offensive to the surrounding culture than blacks and whites worshipping together in the Bible Belt during the pre–civil rights era. Paul is saying the label of Christ now has primacy over the label of white or black or Hispanic or Asian. This is only proven true where it is practiced. So here at the Summit, we are striving hard to diversify our gospel family, not because we want to be politically correct, but because the more diverse a group of people are, the more powerful the explanation is of what brings them together. And we want to give a great case for the power of the gospel to bring deep, family-level unity to a diverse group of people.

Gospel Distinctive: Care

I have three kids, but by the time you read this book, I'll probably have four. Including a baby we lost to miscarriage, my wife has been pregnant for basically five of the last six years, and none of those pregnancies have been easy. Needless to say, it has been a physically and emotionally draining season for us. We are incredibly blessed by the support we have around us. Both sets of grandparents live an hour away, and both are almost always willing to help when needed. I certainly do not take that for granted. We also have an incredible small group and church family who has loved us and sacrificed countless nights so that Courtney and I can preserve our marriage through this season. Our fifth anniversary was possible because a couple in our group came over and watched our oldest while we got away for an overnight trip. Date nights have been possible only because of a few women in our group who've basically become another set of aunts to our kids through so many nights putting them to bed over the years. I thank God regularly for how my gospel family sacrificially cares for my wife, kids, and me.

Through this I've experienced the compassion and care given to us by Christ in His death and resurrection. In the gospel our deepest needs are provided for us when there was no way we could provide for ourselves. When sin created a chasm between God and His people far too wide for us to bridge, He came and got us because He loved enough to care for us. He didn't stop there. When Christ left, He sent the Holy Spirit to care for us, and the Holy Spirit's primary means of caring for us is by mobilizing us to care for one another. When Paul said, "Bear one another's burdens, and so fulfill the law of Christ" (Gal. 6:2), he stated that the application of the gospel (the law of Christ) is the care of fellow Christians. That's why a couple of verses later, he writes, "So then, as we have opportunity, let us do good to everyone, and especially those who are of the household of faith" (Gal. 6:10). A very important tangible application of the gospel is the intentional care you give to others. When you provide care, you are rehearsing the gospel both to yourself and to those for whom you are caring.

Moreover, a family doesn't wait on you to communicate your needs, does it? No. Families assume they are the ones designated to meet your needs until someone tells them to stop. That's usually why in-laws get such a bad rap. Because their "just trying to help" is sometimes received as "all up in my business." Like it or not, it's not a bad model for us as a gospel family. We should be perceptive to the needs of our brothers and sisters and anxious to meet them. So be proactive and intentional in how you seek to meet the needs of those in your gospel family. Think about it. Wouldn't you be much happier having so many people looking out for you that you had to actually turn away help? Anyone would take that over sitting at home alone crying and wondering if anyone cares, as you sink under the weight of your burdens. Just sayin'.

Your rebuttal may be, how is this different from any friendship? The difference is what drives our care for one another. Even when a family member hurts you, you still care for them. In fact, nowhere will the gospel be clearer than when you care for someone who doesn't deserve it. The gospel family never says things like, "Man, I know you'd do the same for me." Because our relationship isn't built on a mutual-care social contract. We say, "Just doing for you what Christ did for me," because our relationship is built on a one-way divine covenant. So there is great security in the gospel family because Christ's unchanging, undeserved love for us is the model for how we love one another.

A NEW BODY

Perhaps the most challenging metaphor for a gospel community to put into practice is that of the body, because of the obvious depth of unity involved. Again, the apostle Paul explains this idea in a couple of places, one being Romans 12:4–5:

> *For as in one body we have many members, and the members do not all have the same function, so we, though many, are one body in Christ, and individually members one of another.*

If you are at all familiar with church and the Bible, you've probably heard the Church referred to as "the body of Christ." The human body is made up of many parts and when they are all healthy, the body functions properly and can do amazing things that no other species can do. We marvel at the dexterity, power, and fitness of professional athletes who spend their lives working hard to get their bodies healthy and finely tuned so they can amaze us with their talents. The one thing all athletes fear, regardless of their sport, is injury because they know it only takes an injury to one part of the body to put the entire body on the sidelines.

I will never forget watching Kevin Ware, a guard for Louisville's 2013 NCAA-championship basketball team, come down after a routine attempt at blocking a shot during the regional final of the NCAA tourney. When he landed on his feet, after jumping to block the shot, his leg snapped in half, and the bone came right out of the skin. The injury was so gruesome that CBS only replayed it once before pulling the clip from on air. Players were crying just looking at the injury. Thankfully, he only suffered a severe broken leg, but it kept him from playing the rest of the tournament.

Think about how all the parts of the body work together to make a basketball player successful. His hands and eyes must be coordinated. His feet must follow his eyes. His ears keep him in tune to what is happening around him. He needs every part of the body to play. Every person needs every body part to function properly to feel healthy. And when one part is not working well, we go see someone who can fix it.

God calls the Church a body because He wants us to understand how integral we are in each other's lives. "Body life" is not optional for any body part. How we choose to function with one another will determine if our one body will be healthy and fruitful or just injury prone. I think the body metaphor highlights two gospel distinctives that, put to work, can bring life and purpose to the members of our local gospel communities.

Gospel Distinctive: Humility

The verse preceding Paul's illustration of the Church as the body of Christ in Romans 12:4–5 reads, "For by the grace given to me I say to everyone among you not to think of himself more highly than he ought to think, but to think with sober judgment, each according to the measure of faith that God has assigned" (v. 3). Paul reminds us that when we begin to think about what our purpose is in the body, pride will be afforded an opportunity to strike. Humility must prevail in our hearts if the body has a chance to be healthy. In 1 Corinthians 12, Paul says that every body part is equally valuable to the body. He tells us that it is absurd to think that one body part is more important than another.

Pastors need to hear this reminder more than anyone else in the gospel community. Paul equates body parts to gifts and acknowledges that each member of the body of Christ has been given a gift to be used for the purpose of making the body function properly. For example, the gift of teaching could be like an arm. So as you teach faithfully, God uses that gift to keep the church body healthy just like a healthy arm serves its role in the human body. Each individual is, in Paul's metaphor, a body part. So humble yourself, knowing that whether you have the gift of teaching, hospitality, or any other gift, you are just a body part. Body parts don't envy. They don't brag. They just do what the brain tells them to do for the good of the body. You need the other members of your body. Seek to serve the body with your gifts, and be ready to help others serve with theirs.

Gospel Distinctive: Unity

Unity is a magnet to which non-Christians are drawn. They want to be a part of community because that desire is in their design. In the gospel body, they have a glimpse into the deeply unified community they've longed for.

There is unity in a human body. Though its parts are diverse, it moves in one direction and works together to accomplish its tasks. This is one of the most fragile but vital components to being a healthy gospel community. Unity will sustain a body of believers through even the most difficult of times. Unity is the building block of growth. When a gospel community starts to operate like a unified body with a common objective, it unlocks the power of transformation for those involved.

This distinctive is last because all the other distinctives work together to build toward this one. The more the others are practiced, the more there will be unity among the believers. There is one key to this though: the Holy Spirit. He brings unity to a body of believers. Paul explains it this way:

> *I therefore, a prisoner for the Lord, urge you to walk in a manner worthy of the calling to which you have been called, with all humility and gentleness, with patience, bearing with one another in love, eager to maintain the unity of the Spirit in the bond of peace. There is one body and one Spirit—just as you were called to the one hope that belongs to your call—one Lord, one faith, one baptism, one God and Father of all, who is over all and through all and in all. But grace was given to each one of us according to the measure of Christ's gift.* (Eph. 4:1–7)

There is one body and one Spirit that unites that body. Christ gave the Holy Spirit to the believers as a guide after He left. It is this guide that empowers, enables, and unifies life in a gospel community. That means we must be eager to entrust the gospel body to God Himself through regular prayer. We must be eager to maintain unity, and beyond that to defend it. We must run to places where a battle wages to disrupt the unity of a local body of believers. Sins like gossip, slander, deceit, etc., are like fires in the church. We must put them out quickly or they will consume everything around them. The gospel is our weapon against the destructive fire of sin. Let us be vigilant in attacking sin with the overwhelming power of the gospel. The Enemy knows there is nothing less effective for advancing God's agenda on the earth than a disunified local church. So as leaders and members of your gospel community, be eager to maintain the unity you have in Christ.

The gospel must be at the center of any group of believers. When it is, we open ourselves to a powerful experience of the community we are created for and for God to begin to do powerful works in and through us. The people of God are marked by these gospel distinctives:

- *Grace:* We forgive much because we have been for-given much in Christ.
- *Generosity:* We give to one another in response to what we were given in Christ.
- *Diversity:* Our family reflects a gospel that recon-ciles races under Christ.
- *Care:* We serve one another joyfully as we've been served by Christ.

74

- *Humility:* We submit to one another in participation with Christ.
- *Unity:* We fight together for oneness in obedience to Christ.

There is no church that has ever or will ever perfectly live out its calling to portray the image of God Himself. Churches are filled with sinners, you and me included. Yet God created this people, the Church, to declare something about Himself even in our imperfection. These distinctives give words to the image of Christ that the watching world sees when it looks at the Church. The church is the visible expression of the gospel. Now let's dive into how that moves from a theological premise to an everyday practice.

DISCUSSION QUESTIONS

1. What sets apart gospel community from other forms of community expressed in our culture?

2. How is your community in your church distinctive from other communities in your context?

3. How do you hope your community will grow to distinguish itself in the future?

CHAPTER 4

ASKING THE RIGHT QUESTIONS

Every human being walks around with an innate desire to find significant belonging. Starbucks tapped into this idea when they coined the 2004–2006 mission statement, "We desire to provide a place where one can find connection so significant that it changes the quality of their lives. Our goal isn't just to provide a great coffee product, but a communal experience." Opening more than 1,300 new stores every year, Starbuck's success is due to having tapped into a fact about people, rooted in their fundamental design. What underlines the philosophical business practice of Starbucks is an anthropological conviction they have about their customers' desires. Everything they do, from the arrangement and decoration of their stores to the design of their coffee cups, is filtered through this mission.

As we discussed in the previous chapters, human beings were created in the image of God who has eternally existed in community and, because of this reality, were created *to* eternally exist in community. God's purpose is not just that we would belong to one another, but that through our belonging God might accomplish His larger purposes, namely His glory. This theological conviction should be the shaping force behind our view of community in the church.

Community is not the goal in the mission of God; bringing Himself glory through the making of disciples is the goal. Community is the primary context God designed to take the church there.

Most of the challenges faced when trying to build a gospel-centered-groups culture in church stems, not from a lack of helpful answers, but from an abundance of asking the wrong questions. In many churches, this will take on a programmatic look and feel. Ministries get created, branded, and communicated in a way to steer people effectively toward involvement (not in and of itself a bad thing). In this pattern, though, success is typically defined numerically (by how many people are involved). When shaping the community culture in a church, the focus needs to move away from creating new programs that lead people to connection and toward placing people into communal relationships that lead to life transformation. This movement starts first with asking the why questions about building community, instead of just the hows. The why questions are the material that builds the foundation (theology) for community in your church.

This foundation should shape your ministry structure (philosophy), which then informs your practice (methodology). Don't be fooled; most of us who operate in and around ministry development would readily say that the Bible is what provides our direction. Yet this isn't what we typically see in churches. What steers the rudder of many churches today is fear fueled by consumerism, rather than courage fueled by truth. To build a gospel-centered-groups ministry in the life of your church, you will need to build a firm theological foundation on convictional leadership.

FOUNDATION, NOT FORMULA

One of the great joys I (Trevor) get to experience on a regular basis is to consult with churches from all over the map both geographically and denominationally. A few years ago, a very large and well-known church sent a team of researchers to come and interview a few members of our staff. The topic of the conversation was "reaching the next generation." This particular church has had a long history of growth and trendsetting but recently began to experience a sharp decline in people under the age of thirty-five in their congregation. The lead team of this church assembled a group of researchers to go and interview several churches across the nation whose congregations were made up largely of younger generations (eighteen to thirty-two years old).

During our two days together I'm pretty sure I walked away with more insight than they did. Much of our conversation went like this:

Other Church: "I noticed you have your preschool ministry at the front of your building, so it is the first thing you see when you walk in. Was that done to demonstrate a priority around younger children in the life of your church?"

Me: "No, we built our church in a grocery store and had limited options."

Other Church: "I noticed that there are no windows or natural light coming into your sanctuary. Was this done to create a more meditational or concert feel during your worship services?"

Me: "No, we built our church in a grocery store and had limited options."

Other Church: "I noticed that you could see all of the entrances into your weekend ministries from the foyer (preschool, elementary, and sanctuary). Was that done to make all of them appear to be equal in importance?"

Me: "No, we built our church in a grocery store and had limited options."

Now, don't get me wrong, we have incredibly talented people on our staff who had great intentions designing our facility. People who are wired in ways I could never begin to understand put countless hours of prayer and thought into what our building looks like and how it functions. Can putting a preschool ministry in the front of your building communicate something about how much you value children? Sure it can! However, what goes on in those classrooms, and the quality of leaders who are teaching children week in and week out are of considerable more importance than the positioning of doors and windows.

The conclusion I drew during our time with this church group wasn't that they lacked a genuine eagerness to reach the next generation in their context of ministry. It was that, in their journey to learn, they began by asking the wrong questions. The key to building a biblically faithful ministry doesn't begin with aesthetics but with a theological foundation. What we believe about God and who and what He has created His Church to be and do should be the starting place of your endeavor. Whether you are setting out to build a gospel-centered children's ministry, groups ministry, or serving ministry, a solid theological framework is paramount.

In 2008 we underwent some significant changes in the groups ministry at The Village. Groups at that time were growing in numbers but were lacking in depth. Out of a conviction to see theology inform our philosophy of ministry, we had to attack the tree at its root. That year has become a benchmark year in group life at our church, because it was that year when we said what was going to control the rudder of groups at The Village was a theological understanding of community, not the growing demand for people to connect. Up until that point, supply and demand was the primary motivation for ministry development. Everything was reactionary. The church was growing by the thousands, and thousands also wanted access to groups. In order to react to the demand, an efficient system was built to create supply. You see the misstep here? The driving factor behind how groups were being started was a reaction to satisfy a demand.

Elevating the priority for matching the demand with supply meant success was defined by the number of groups established. This subtle step led to quantity over quality. Now I want to be intentional here to mention that we continue to put very large goals in front of our groups team every year on how many groups to start, and we push hard toward meeting those goals. However, the goals are built on a foundation that is sound and tested. We can cast wide nets to our congregation, inviting people into leadership, because we have built a leadership pipeline around theological values that we believe filter right and necessary things versus being filtered by environmental pressures. Josh Patterson, a contributing author of *Creature of the Word* says, "Drift is subtle."[1] We don't, at the outset of an endeavor, say that we want the wrong things to dictate how ministry is developed in the context of our churches, but slowly we get lulled into making decisions around these pressures, and one day we wake up with a ministry philosophy that is built more around consumerism than conviction.

During that formational year, we put a few stakes in the ground that were really guardrails for us in moving toward building gospel-centered community. These guiding statements were born out of theological convictions and ran contrary to most of the modes of operations of churches our size, such as, "We would rather not have a group to send someone to than send someone to an unhealthy group." Now I don't believe for a moment that anyone would read that statement and fundamentally disagree with what it says. But there is a vast difference between acknowledging that statement to be true and letting statements like that become rudders for ministry direction. For us, this statement led us to clearly define things like:

- How do home groups contribute to making disciples in our context?
- What does a healthy home group strive to be and do in the life of our church?
- What are the primary areas of focus when building these kinds of groups?
- Who is qualified to lead this kind of group?

These shifts led us to a very slow and intentional redirecting of our groups ministry away from a connections strategy to a place that provides a context for discipleship. We did not first seek to answer the question of how to form enough groups to fit all of these people. The answers to questions like that will lead to drifting off mission and toward being a consumer-driven programmatic church.

COURAGE TO LEAD

Recently we were sitting with the leadership team from another church who approached us to consult with them on how to steer their church in a different direction. They believed their church was heading toward rapid decline and had become largely irrelevant, especially among the younger generations. This particular church has been a flagship in its community for decades and until recent years had enjoyed continued success in their context. What impressed me so much about this church was their willingness to ask the difficult questions and receive difficult answers. They, as leadership, had come to the humble place of realizing their trajectory and wanted to steward a change in their congregation for the better.

We spent the better part of our time together unpacking our philosophy of ministry and how we arrived where we are. An important piece of our history is a significant change our leadership led the congregation through a few years ago. In short, the shift was toward clarifying our mission and simplifying our strategy. This move grew out of a conviction from our elders to be more intentional as a church in how we pursue making disciples in our context.

This shift was prompted by theological convictions that led to a philosophical shift and ultimately changed a good deal of the methodology we employed. We wanted to align our strategy with these convictions, which meant that some things we had historically done we would no longer do. We moved away from ministries that were aimed toward health, but did not fit with this aligned strategy, and concentrated our efforts toward the things that we believe more effectively contributed to moving in the direction we were going. Leading the church through this change meant leading them away from many things they had come to enjoy and value. As we walked this group through that two-year process, we gave examples of things like men's and women's Bible studies—which are staple events in most churches—that would not be a part of the new direction.

The change in direction was a very difficult season in the life of our church. But because these changes emanated from a reservoir of theological convictions on disciple making in the life of our church, the conversations and confrontations became opportunities to shepherd our people toward faithfulness to the gospel. Don't get me wrong; some of them were difficult and messy but worth every bit of it.

As we began to unpack situation after situation, one of the men in the other church group was provoked in a good way. You could see the dots connecting in his mind, and he began to dream out loud of what similar changes could look like in their church. As he spoke, one of the other men in their group interrupted him and said, "I agree with where you are going, but if it means having some of these conversations, then leave me out."

The mountain of opposition seemed insurmountable. Building ministry from a theological foundation takes convictional leadership. Andy Stanley, in his book *The Next Generation Leader,* says there are three expressions of courageous leadership: (1) the courage to say no, (2) the courage to face the current reality, and (3) the courage to dream. He quotes Peter Senge: "An accurate and insightful view of current reality is as important as clear vision. Unfortunately, most of us are in the habit of opposing our biases on our perceptions of current reality."[2] Stanley goes on to say, "Designing and implementing a strategy for change is a waste of time until you have discovered and embraced the current reality. If you don't know where you really are, it is impossible to get where you need to be."[3]

Nehemiah gives us a great example of courageous and convictional leadership. In chapter 4 we see Israel taking great opposition in the building of the wall.

> But when Sanballat and Tobiah and the Arabs and the Ammonites and the Ashdodites heard that the repairing of the walls of Jerusalem was going forward and that the breaches were beginning to be closed, they were very angry. And they all plotted together to come and fight against Jerusalem and to cause confusion in it. (Neh. 4:7–8)

The people have a mind to work, this wall will be rebuilt, and they will do it. In the midst of progress, Israel is taking opposition and attack from all sides. Onslaughts come in the form of physical attacks and attempts to create division. The people began to grow weary of the work and complained:

> "The strength of those who bear the burdens is failing. There is too much rubble. By ourselves we will not be

able to rebuild the wall." And our enemies said, "They
will not know or see till we come among them and kill
them and stop the work." (Neh. 4:10–11)

Nehemiah now faces opposition not just externally, but internally. Outside the walls are nations who have mounted efforts to see this project fail. Inside the walls, the hearts of the builders have begun to grow weak and weary. The desire to abandon their mission is elevated to the only option, and this is where Nehemiah steps in.

So in the lowest parts of the space behind the wall,
in open places, I stationed the people by their clans,
with their swords, their spears, and their bows. And
I looked and arose and said to the nobles and to
the officials and to the rest of the people, "Do not
be afraid of them. Remember the Lord, who is great
and awesome, and fight for your brothers, your sons,
your daughters, your wives, and your homes." (Neh.
4:13–14)

Nehemiah begins to make strategic changes, but in doing so calls his people to remember who gave them this mission—He who is great and awesome. The Lord surely will supply them with what they need to carry out His will. Nehemiah calls his people to faithfulness and as a leader employs changes and presses forward out of conviction and courage.

One ironic aspect about leading in the church today is that the bulk of the opposition you face will be internal instead of external. Golden calves that may be obvious to you tend to be far less evident to those for whom they carry significance. As a leader, conviction does not give you license to do whatever you want. If you are leading a ministry, whether as a layperson or paid staff, the Lord has sovereignly placed those people in your care, and you are charged to lovingly shepherd them toward faithfulness, even when they don't want to go.

We recognize the importance of community in the life of a believer because we were first fashioned in the image of a communal God. This, combined with what God has called the Church to be and do together, provides a compelling case for the formation of a groups ministry in your church. There will be many roadblocks and distractions along the way begging you to drift off mission. This is why a theological foundation and practicing convictional leadership are crucial to employ what we discuss throughout this book.

DISCUSSION QUESTIONS

1. What questions do you ask to evaluate community in the life of your church?

2. What questions should you ask?

3. How can asking the right questions help your people grow?

CHAPTER 5

THE MISSING LINK: ALIGNMENT

THE GREAT CONFUSION

Chuck and Yolanda arrive at your church for your weekend service. They drop their kids off with the kids' ministry just like they have each time since they started attending six weeks ago. As they walk into the service, they are greeted and maybe even handed a piece of paper with some information about happenings in your church. For 60 to 90 minutes (or longer if you roll that way) they experience your church. Songs about the resurrection, a sermon on prayer, and announcements about a food drive are all communicating to them what your church is about.

When the service is over, they go pick up their kids, who tell them all about Moses and the frog plague, and head home. On the drive home they decide it's time to finally check out a small group. Brandon and Ashley lead a small group in their area. The group is finishing up a book about how Jesus makes you crazy for His mission overseas. At the end of their weekly Tuesday night gathering Brandon asks, "What would you guys like to study next?" The answers vary so Brandon says he will pray about it and check some websites. Chuck and Yolanda hang out for a while and then head home, planning to repeat their church cocktail of Sunday morning worship and Tuesday night small group. In the three to four hours of time Chuck and Yolanda spent with your church this week, their family interacted with the resurrection, prayer, a food drive, Moses, and a crazed missiologist. And next week they will likely interact with an entirely new buffet of content.

Based on our collective interaction with many churches, we've found the above description to be somewhat accurate of what a typical church experience is like in our day. It is a fragmented form of discipleship where the church attender is barraged with a myriad of unrelated ideas on a weekly basis, and is left trying to make sense of the pieces. While we say we are fulfilling the great commission, many of our people are experiencing the great confusion.

As leaders in our church, we can offer people a host of varied experiences with little direction as to where those experiences are taking them. To use a biblical illustration: the leaders of the church are its shepherds. Herding sheep involves getting all of the sheep going in the same direction toward a common destination. Can you imagine if a group of shepherds responsible for one flock were each shouting differing directions to the sheep? Though they all had the same destination in mind, what would the sheep think? In the chaos they wouldn't know where to go, which probably means they wouldn't go anywhere. If we want to take a group of people somewhere, we've got to have a clear, unified plan of where we are going and how we are going to get there.

THE POWER OF ALIGNMENT

This chapter addresses an opportunity I believe many church families are missing. It is a critical component that can be either a significant hurdle or a game-changing catalyst to becoming disciple-making churches. At my church, we call it alignment.

Alignment is the intentional coordination of all disciple-making efforts to create a clear discipleship path for the church. In a church where alignment is practiced, weekend worship teams, kids and student ministries, small groups, local outreach, and global missions are all clear on the mission of the church and the way their ministry contributes to it this week, this month, and this year. In a church with only one leader, alignment is likely built in. After all, coordinating with yourself shouldn't be too difficult! Once another leader is in the mix the game changes and alignment becomes something you have to intentionally work at.

Truthfully, the goal is not to introduce a new idea, but maybe to awaken you to the reality of where you've drifted to and call you back to where you started. Aligning ministry efforts is often much like aligning the steering in a car. You have to get your alignment checked because your car will slip out of alignment in a subtle, almost indiscernible way. Next thing you know you've veered off the road and you're in a ditch. It's not a sudden, jerky move toward the ditch; it's a slow and subtle one. And just because you fixed it once doesn't mean it will never go out of alignment again. The alignment on your car needs to be checked and rechecked. Normal, healthy car maintenance is to check your alignment often.

So regardless of what level of leadership you are in, as you read through this chapter, think of this as a ministry alignment tune-up. Go ahead and do the hard work of putting your pride down. Like I said, my intent is not to blow your mind, but to challenge your status quo. We'll talk in a moment about what alignment looks like, but first here are some of the benefits we've seen from it.

Unity

In Ephesians 4 the apostle Paul calls the church family to pursue unity. He urges us to be eager to maintain unity in the Spirit. The reality is, it is so easy for a bunch of sinners to get bogged down in the weeds of secondary and tertiary matters. Our sin nature leaves us with a predisposed bias against unity and toward protecting our precious self-interests at all costs. This deadly combination results in each individual believing his or her own preferences or passions should be the driving focus of the church. Alignment helps keep the mission of the church in front of itself at every level from weekend worship to the living room on Tuesday night. When our pastor preaches on the same biblical principles our groups are applying, there is a heightened sense of unity among our church family. Unity is difficult to quantify, but signs of it are clearly evident.

Our church recently underwent a season focusing on generosity, during which all ministries were aligned around generosity as the focal point. Listening to our leaders talk about how their group members were praying and working through what they were being challenged with was incredibly rewarding. Experiencing our church unite and commit themselves to living generously for the sake of the gospel was *awe-inspiring*. Disunity is usually the consequence of a lack of common mission. Mission doesn't create unity in the Church; the Holy Spirit does. However, a group aligned around a clear mission creates a much healthier environment for the Holy Spirit to bring unity to that group.

Momentum

When everyone finally becomes unified around one compelling mission, momentum builds and results begin to appear. We've discovered that when the parents and kids in a family are all interacting with the same biblical principles, it creates a greenhouse for parents to grow into disciple makers of their kids. When we clarified small groups as our one vehicle for discipleship, we saw small-group involvement go from below 30 percent to above 60 percent of our weekend attendance, even as weekend attendance grew by 25 percent every year. Momentum builds on itself. The way I phrase this to our staff team is clarity in expectations creates confidence in execution. More and more people are moving from observers to participants in the mission of God, in part because they understand what the mission of God means and looks like in their church.

Care

Once everyone is clear on how you are going to structure discipleship, they begin to invest their time and energy toward improving the quality of care they provide one another. For the Summit, small groups became the discipleship environment we began pointing everyone toward. Aligning all of our shepherding efforts in one primary direction was a key decision. Other supporting decisions followed. We incorporated all of our elders into our small-group coaching team. Now our elders, the people we believe God has gifted to watch over the church, primarily function as small-group coaches. One of our best decisions came when we hired a pastor of counseling. We hired him into the small-groups team so his ministry energy could be harnessed in the environment where the majority of soul care takes place in our church: small groups. Our incredible first-time guest team began selling small groups from the moment someone came on site. Now the most common question you hear on the weekend is either "Where is your bathroom?" or "Are you in a small group?" I'll come back to the nuts and bolts of this in just a bit. I want you to catch the idea here: the quality of care we were able to give our people improved in direct proportion to the amount we aligned our capacity to care.

Impact

Possibly the greatest way we've seen alignment increase our effectiveness is in the impact some of our people are having locally and around the world. Now that they have a sense of confidence of what discipleship is and how we will support them to do it, many have taken what we started to heights we never imagined. I never dreamed of small groups in Spanish, Chinese, and Arabic. But having experienced the model of small group, some of our leaders native to those languages took the initiative to begin groups for non-English speakers.

The other day one of our pastors asked me if it was okay that he was starting a Summit small group in a prison. A prison! To my shame it never even occurred to me to dream in that direction, yet a group of people caught the idea that the gospel carried along by a community built around it can change lives. So they took that to the prison and are seeing men and women come to Christ there.

Recently, we took a season and aligned our entire church around evangelism and the mission of God because we recognized, while our people were excited about Jesus, they didn't really know how to talk about Him. The following year 35 percent of our small groups saw someone they knew come to know Christ, and we baptized twice as many people as we did the year before. When we aligned our small-group multiplication strategy with our church-planting strategy, we began sending larger teams out from our church more frequently.

Aligning all of your disciple-making efforts along common values and initiatives is a powerful step that requires zero dollars and can be done at any level of any church of any size.

HOW IT WORKS PART 1: ALIGNING WEEKEND WORSHIP AND SMALL GROUPS

To preserve our focus, I'm going to confine this discussion to small groups. It is important to note, however, that these ideas can be translated to other areas of ministry.

Let's start by acknowledging two truths:

1. The worship gathering is not more important than the small-group gathering.
2. The small-group gathering is not more important than the worship gathering.

Both the weekend worship gathering and the small group should be environments in which you are aligning toward your goal of making disciples. If you do not incorporate them both, as equals, into your strategy, you will likely encounter frustration with the rest of what we are getting at in this book. Once you see them as two assets to accomplishing the same goal, then you can leverage those assets to maximize your effectiveness in disciple making. Here's how this works practically in our setting.

As in most churches, mission and vision come from the sermon. Those gifted by God to preach and shepherd the church preach from the Scriptures each weekend. Because we believe they are gifted by God to lead the church, we want to give significant weight to the sermons they preach. What we realized, however, is that most people forget almost everything they heard from a sermon within 48 hours. So we leverage our small groups by having them discuss and apply the same biblical principles they learned on the weekend. No, I wasn't the first guy to think of this. Some friends in ministry were already doing it and told us about it. The Dutch Reformed did it in the nineteenth century, the Puritans did it, and, if you look at Acts 2, the first church did it as well. Discipleship isn't about being inventive but being faithful and effective. We quickly found this to be an effective way to improve how we make disciples at our church.

Normally on Wednesday morning someone from our groups team sits in with whomever is preaching that weekend to hear what the message is going to be about. The team member will consult with the preacher and other team members about the best angle to take in the small-group discussion for the week. The goal is not to have the group go through the same Bible passage, but to engage Scripture on the same core principles. The team member will then write a study that seeks to dig into a different but parallel passage of Scripture. That study is sent out to our leaders by Thursday afternoon and they send it on to their members so that everyone in a group has a chance to engage it before the weekend message. The group members listen actively to the message and then go into their groups prepared to move toward the application of content they've now engaged once or twice already.

Roughly twice a year we go through an alignment series as an entire church. We plan these out months in advance and try to develop a unifying theme from a place in Scripture that our sermons and small-group discussion will be able to dig into. We give study guides to everyone at the beginning of the series and usually incorporate stories and challenges into the small-group experience. We've been aligning the weekend with the week for more than five years and have received great feedback from our leaders and members.

If that sounds like overkill to you, let me assure you that aligning small groups to your weekend is not something you need a small-groups team to do. In fact, I've found this is one of the easiest strategies that I can teach church planters. I tell them to think of the one or two main points of the message and a supporting passage of Scripture to the one they are teaching from. All that's left to do is write up three or four questions based on those main points. E-mail or post it for your leaders and you are done! My good friend

Logan Keck is a church planter in Boston. He's the only staff member of his church right now, and he does this exercise on a regular basis. He and other pastors have told me this exercise actually makes their sermons better because it helps them think like their listeners when prepping their message.

Here are some other practical benefits to implementing a model that aligns the worship gathering and the small-group time:

- **Bigger recruiting pool for leaders.** "We'll prep your study if you will care for your people" is a pretty good recruiting line in our setting. It doesn't mean we don't want leaders studying the Bible, it simply means that we don't ask them to be Bible experts. We want them to be shepherds. Review chapter 1 for more on shepherd-leaders.

- **Easier for new people to plug in.** For those who connect first to your weekend services, they are able to pick up right where a small group is. This is especially helpful for new Christians or non-Christians who might be intimidated walking into a room full of people neck-deep in Leviticus.

- **Improved learning experience.** By interacting with the material multiple times in different formats, small-group members get a richer and deeper learning experience than we were giving them in the buffet approach to learning.[1]

HOW IT WORKS PART 2: CREATING A CLEAR DISCIPLESHIP PATH

Aligning your worship gatherings to your small groups is a great start, but it will only get you so far. To achieve the unity, momentum, care, and impact you want as a church you cannot stop there. If you do, you run the risk of creating a leadership base that is too dependent on the weekend service. I believe we want to develop shepherd-leaders who grow into partners in disciple making. I don't want to plan every question for a small-group leader to ask for the next twenty-five years of his or her life. I want them to grow into people who can recognize those spiritual-growth moments in both individuals and groups and speak gospel truth without hesitation. I want the legacy of our church to be that we made disciple makers of multiple generations. Sermon alignment is a tool to this greater end.

To get there, you are going to have to train people to make disciples. You are going to have to be clear on both what a disciple is and the process of making one. To be brutally honest, this is where it gets hard for me. We are trying to build a path that is flexible enough for leaders to feel empowered, while structured enough that it can maintain a clear identity.

With this in mind, some of our pastoral team took a full-day, off-site retreat to figure out what we meant by discipleship and how we would communicate it clearly to our people. After hours of caffeine-infused discussion, we came up with a system we've stood with to this day. We call it "The Wheel" and we use it as our discipleship "path." Here is how we explain it:

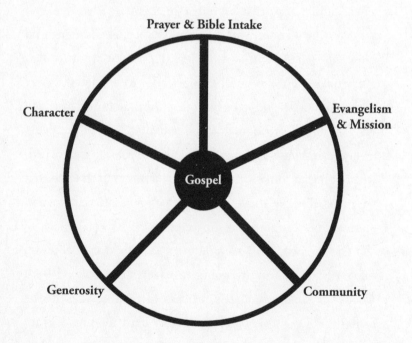

The Wheel is an exercise on discipleship in a gospel-centered life. The inward renewal the gospel brings is represented at the center of the wheel diagram. The five spokes of the wheel represent the outward signs of this renewal. The purpose of this exercise is to diagnose one's spiritual health, reveal underlying beliefs, and promote gospel-motivated transformation.

The Center of the Wheel

Before we are to do anything else, we are called to love God. That is the greatest commandment (Matt. 22:37–39). Love, however, cannot be forced. It is the voluntary aligning of one's affections onto that which one desires most. We love God not because we have to, but because we want to. When this happens, we experience a new kind of obedience to His commands. We find the source of such love in the gospel where Jesus died for our sins to restore us to God our Father. The Christian life is a joyful response to who God is, which is most clearly revealed in what He has done for us in the death and resurrection of Jesus Christ. If you have not trusted Christ for your salvation and surrendered to His authority over your life, start there before going any further.

The Spokes of the Wheel

1. Prayer and Bible Intake: The pursuit of God by getting to know Him through the Bible. It involves setting time apart specifically to reflect on who God is from His Word and to talk to Him through prayer. The rest of the Christian life flows from this unceasing communion with God.

2. Community: Christian community means your life and faith is not kept to yourself. It is lived out in gospel-centered relationships with other believers who encourage, exhort, and correct one another. Moreover, Christian community involves using your gifts, talents, and passions to help serve people inside and outside the church.

3. Evangelism and Missions: *Evangelism* is motivated by the belief that the gospel is the good news that people from all backgrounds believe so that they might be saved from death and live in new life. From Scripture we see that He's given us the power (Acts 1:8) and the mandate to witness firsthand others coming to follow Him (Rom. 10:14). *Missions* is an advancement of evangelism in two fronts, local and global. Locally, God appointed the local church to care for the poor and oppressed in its community. Globally, we acknowledge the best way to care for a community is through planting thriving local churches.

4. Generosity: Christians give generously of their time, resources, money, and energy as an act of thanksgiving for all God has given us. Our generosity does not flow from legalistic obligations, guilt, or fear. Rather, it flows from the life-altering realization that God was exceedingly generous with us by sending His Son to die for us, and all we have is a gracious gift He has given us.

5. Character: To grow in character means to become increasingly more like Christ in one's thoughts, words, deeds, and way of life. From the moment of our salvation, God is working in us and through us to bring our life more and more into conformity with the perfect character of our Lord Jesus Christ.

> Warning: The Enemy would use such an exercise to make you feel shamed and condemned by God. If that happens, run away from this exercise quickly. Think of this more like a workout program than a beat down. In a workout you feel pain, but it's worth it because you desire the end result of a healthier life. A workout with no results is just a beat down. *Nobody likes a beat down.*

Each week you will have a self-evaluation to complete before coming to small group. You will not be required to share your answers with your group, but an assessment is a healthy way to prepare your heart and mind to be challenged in this area.

Each Wheel *spoke* is accompanied by three categories of questions designed to gauge the health of a believer in that area.

- Where are you?
- Why are you there?
- What can we do to help you grow?

1. Where are you? Your response should be drawn from the concrete evidence seen in your life. For example, it is hard to be self-delusional about how strong your prayer life is if you have not prayed in a month. Some of the evaluation questions are open-ended and others on a 1–10 scale. While such a scale is not perfect, it does provide a simple starting point to move on from.

2. Why are you there? This question is intended to connect your actions with your beliefs. The goal is to remove the "dream" one has about oneself and deal with the reality of what one believes at a practical level. For example, one may say they believe in the Great Commission, but over the last year they have not told anybody about how Christ rescued them. The goal is to reveal that something else (maybe comfort, security, pride) is dictating their daily life more than the gospel. At this stage you must understand that your actions flow from your true beliefs. This is the key. Remember, these actions we are talking about are signs of a renewed heart and mind. *The most important question to lead you toward gospel-centered life change is why.*

3. What can we do to help you grow? This question is to help you with steps toward growing in belief and action according to the gospel. Question 1 observes one's actual life in Christ. Question 2 reveals what one's true motivation is. Each week's group discussion includes a chance for you to answer this question in your group time.

Where do we use the Wheel? At the small-group level we train leaders to evaluate group health using the Wheel. We give them 40 percent of the year where they are in charge of deciding what the study aspect of their small group will be. In consultation with their coach (every leader has a coach), the leader decides which spoke of the wheel he or she needs to drill down on with the group. How does this match with the sermon-alignment idea? We call it the 40/40/20 rule (very creative I know, but it helps us break down the weekly meeting part of small group life):

- 40 percent of the year all groups align together with weekend services in an alignment series mentioned above

- 40 percent of the year group leaders are free to use the Wheel to determine what their group should focus on
- 20 percent of the year we leave open as a buffer for things like Christmas, sickness, vacation, etc.

I hope you do not see anything revolutionary in the Wheel. Its simplicity is what helps us use it across so many different settings with our people. The more people we can equip to lead others on a discipleship trajectory that we believe is faithful to the Scriptures and effective in moving people along, the better!

Before we move on, let's quickly review. Alignment is the intentional coordination of all disciple-making efforts to create a clear discipleship path for the church. For us at the Summit, putting the alignment principle into practice takes two forms. We align our weekend worship gatherings with our small groups. We also align our leaders around a common discipleship path we call the Wheel.

WHAT CAN KNOCK YOU OUT OF ALIGNMENT

As we said at the beginning of the chapter, this is kind of like a checkup for your group or church. Maybe this compels you to do the painful work of self-reflection to see where you may be drifting out of alignment. I hope what you are seeing throughout this chapter is that alignment isn't complex but it is hard work. Retaining a simple, clear direction at every level of your organization doesn't happen accidentally. It requires time, energy, and coordination—all of which will require some level of sacrifice from any number of people. Here are two things to watch out for as you work toward alignment.

Unclear Communication

Best-selling leadership author Patrick Lencioni said in his book *The Advantage* that an organization's health is its most valuable asset in achieving success. Health, he goes on to say, is created through clarity. At every level of the organization, there must be absolute clarity in what the entire organization is out to accomplish. In fact, three of his four steps to help you become a healthy organization are creating, maintaining, and reinforcing clarity in your communication.[2] For many churches and groups there isn't too much ambiguity in what their purpose is: make disciples. The breakdown happens when leadership communicates the strategy they will use to accomplish their purpose. One helpful question to keep in front of you is what is the win for someone in your church family. When they _____, you feel like that is a win. If there is more than one, what are they and how do they fit together? Work hard to develop this clarity. Here was our mission statement when we started this process:

Bringing fame to God through passionate worship, discipling everyone from our neighborhood to the nations, connecting members to ministry, and building everything on the foundation of prayer.

There was nothing bad about it, but do you think our people could repeat it? Our staff couldn't recall it! Which means despite the great wording, we weren't giving our people a clear direction. In one of our first waves of aligning, we took a page from a book called *Simple Church*[3] and went for a clearer way to say what we were already saying. Now our mission statement is:

Love God, Love Each Other, Love Our World

Nothing special, just clear. And clear sticks with people. A mission statement alone doesn't make disciples, but it helped give us a common reference point.

If you are a small-group leader, seek out this type of clarity from leadership. Remember, clarity in expectations creates confidence in execution. If you get nothing else out of this chapter, let it be that you need to fight hard for clarity in everything that you ask of your people. But, I hope you get more than that.

Overprogramming

If you want to really raise up leaders, you need to give them room to lead. That means you have to give enough structure to point everyone in the same direction while leaving room for leaders to take ownership over the vision. Leaders will execute your idea; they will own their ideas. You want owners. You want people who are texting you new dreams about how they can accomplish God's mission in their context as a part of your team. That's why we only program about 40 percent, or sixteen weeks, where we really ask leaders to align closely with the church. Those seasons are our alignment series mentioned previously. Give leaders a wide but clear track to run on and the space to own it, and see what happens! If you are thinking, "man that is messy," you are right, it is messy. Church is messy. It is a bunch of sinners trying to love and care for each other. But isn't it worth navigating the mess?

HOW TO GET STARTED

If you are ready to walk through alignment with your church, group, or organization, let me start you with a few first steps.

1. Pray. How often do we as leaders jump the gun with something that seems like a good idea before letting God guide us in it? Ask God for guidance in how you can best lead His people. Let Him guide you in building an alignment strategy.

2. Define the win. Here are some sample questions to get you started:

- What is your current strategy for making disciples?
- What are you trying to accomplish through small groups?
- Are there nonnegotiable components to your strategy? What are they?
- What is a disciple?
- How do/could all of your discipleship environments work better toward a common goal?

3. Write it down and then revise it. It will be much easier to communicate an idea to someone else if you write it down and look at it. Just write down everything that comes to mind. Then take the time to make some sense of it. Got any teachers in your group or church? Ask for their help in communicating what you believe God is leading you toward. If this seems trivial, remember that words matter.

4. Beta test. Before trying it out in the pulpit on the weekend, spend some time talking through it with key leaders you trust. Invite them into the process of alignment. For example, if you decide to align the sermon with the small-group discussion, try it out on a group or two before making it the "new thing." This will give you the chance to tweak both practice and language before implementing on a larger scale. This step is especially important for larger churches who will devote more time and resources to making major shifts.

5. Scale your implementation plan. The last people to hear about this new plan should be Chuck and Yolanda. All of your leadership should already know about it and have had the chance to ask questions. When your leaders are clear on what is happening, implementation will go a lot smoother.

YOU AREN'T THAT SMART ANYWAY

One thing I (Spence) want to leave you with in this chapter is the reminder that spiritual growth isn't a science. I used to get so frustrated as a small-groups pastor when the people in our church weren't all uniformly growing spiritually according to the formula I'd laid out for them.

A few years in ministry taught me that spiritual growth just doesn't work that way. Spiritual growth is messy to us because the real power for transformation belongs to the Holy Spirit, whom we cannot control. In other words, as clever as my system can be, I'm not God. I'm a sinful finite being trying to disciple other sinful finite beings. And so are you. If you wait until you've crafted the perfect discipleship strategy to get started, you'll be waiting until Jesus comes back. In the meantime, just get started making disciples as faithfully as you can and trust God with the giant gap between your brain and His. I think you'll find that gap will become the space where God stretches you to trust Him with your people.

DISCUSSION QUESTIONS

1. Does your church currently have an aligned discipleship strategy?

2. What are the benefits of alignment?

3. Since spiritual growth is not a science, how can we take that into account as we develop vision and leadership strategy?

CHAPTER 6

GOSPELING ONE ANOTHER

Take care, brothers, lest there be in any of you an
evil, unbelieving heart, leading you to fall away from
the living God. But exhort one another every day,
as long as it is called "today," that none of you may
be hardened by the deceitfulness of sin. For we have
come to share in Christ, if indeed we hold our origi-
nal confidence firm to the end.

HEBREWS 3:12–14

I (Spence) began a new workout routine a few months ago that is unlike anything I've done before. It is a group-oriented workout where ten or so of us show up uncomfortably early a couple times a week to take our beating. We attempt a series of intense muscle confusion exercises that leave me writhing on the ground, wondering from what kind of third-world terrorist prisons the creators of this whole miserable concept emerged. As a group, we all complete the same exercises, each attempting to outdo the other in how fast we can finish the workout of the day.

What I love (or at least, have grown to appreciate) about this style of workout is that we are experiencing these blistering morning workouts together, creating a team mentality for the group. We are all enduring the same brutality *together*, shouting at one another to keep going and the workout isn't over until every last one of us is finished. We've got a common language, a workout language that we all use to push one another beyond our breaking points. "Keep it up!" "Only ___ more!" and "PUSH!" are common encouragements I hear when everything in me screams, "STOP RUNNING YOU FOOL, YOU'RE GOING TO DIE!"

Can I be brutally honest for a moment? If not for the communal aspect of this workout, 7:00 a.m. on workout days would sooner find me eating a Grand Slam platter at our local Waffle House (bacon, eggs, waffles, hashbrowns, and coffee) than throwing eighteen-pound medicine balls twelve feet high, one hundred times in a row (yeah, we do that). Left to my own devices, I am indeed prone to wander— right toward the smell of fried food. Similarly, if not for the communal aspect of the way that I have chosen to live my life, I would be much more easily enticed by the allure of sin than by the unglamorous, daily work of fighting it.

As believers, we are called to live our lives *together*, but I think we are missing the workout language. If God designed people as His "Plan A" for communicating His truth, then we need to begin speaking to one another more intentionally. Oh we've got plenty of tired Christian platitudes. We call those "Christianese" in our church. You know, those sayings that end up on rural church signs: "You think it's hot here"; or, "Drugs leave you senseless, liquor leaves you breathless, but Jesus won't leave you regardless,"; or, "Don't let the devil ride, cause he'll end up drivin'." I could do this all day, but you get the point.

What we need are the real-life kind of words that we can use to audibly speak the gospel to one another on a continual basis. It is not enough to live alongside one another, simply assuming that we are believing the gospel at all times. To do so runs the risk of forgetting it all together. You and I are built to hear and speak God's truth often and audibly to one another. And according to the author of Hebrews, this daily intervention is our primary weapon against the Enemy's subtle attack on our hearts and minds.

We want to give you some ways to begin infusing the gospel into your speech. We want to move you from knowing about the gospel to fluently speaking the gospel to another person with confidence. To say it simply, we want to equip your local body of believers to begin "gospeling" one another. If you'll allow it, we want you to begin "gospeling" one another. This is where the proverbial rubber meets the road, where you can move from receiving information to practicing biblical community. It's going to be awkward. Introducing this will not be easy, and we'll talk more about that in a minute. But it's worth it.

What if the only thing keeping us from life-giving community was not just believing the gospel, but knowing how to unleash it into our lives? The following are six starter phrases that will help to create gospel intentionality in your conversations with those in your community of believers.

"I've sinned against you, and I'm sorry."

Confession and repentance isn't easy. Apologizing to another human being requires a painful amount of humility. This is why it can be a gospeling moment. When we remember what miserable sinners we are in the eyes of a holy God, there is no room left for pride. There is only one way to get to a place where you can humble yourself to the point of true repentance. You must encounter the God who left the beauty and perfection of heaven to take on skin and bones and walk beside us in our brokenness, the God who took that brokenness on Himself and was nailed to a piece of wood for it. People who have genuinely encountered that God are people consistently marked by deep humility.

The risk in committing to biblical community is that we will become close enough to deeply wound each other. That you will commit sin against another person in the family of God is inevitable. The grueling, worthwhile work of confession and repentance requires two steps.

The first is toward God Himself. When David slept with a married woman, then gave the order for her husband to be murdered, his confession, recorded in Psalm 51:4, was "against you, you only, have I sinned." Really? What about the family you just destroyed, David? Don't you think you sinned against them? God is showing us something deep in David's confession. When we choose our way over God's way, we recommit the same sin Adam made in the garden. So the consequence for us is the same. Just like Adam, our sin creates a separation between God and us. Every moment of sin is a moment of rebellion against God our king. More than hurting our fellow man with our sin, we are hardening ourselves to the God we so desperately need. David understood that his sin affected his relationship with both God and man. Your first step in repentance is to acknowledge that your sin is against God and to confess it to Him.

The second step is to go to the individual and acknowledge your sin to them, not only the action, but also the motivation behind it. Remember; what we believe drives what we do. And in sin, we are not just doing wrong but believing wrong. When we do the painful work of searching our heart for *why* we sinned against another, we get to the root of the sin. Here, down at the root, is where the Holy Spirit can go to work on us to create lasting change.

How do you put this into practice? Once you have confessed your sin to God and turned (repented) from it, you go to your brother or sister. There, you confess and repent to them. It could go something like this:

I'm sorry, I sinned against you when I _____. I did this because _____ and I'm sorry. I've confessed this to God and am now confessing it to you. I hope you will forgive me.

This may seem simple. I hope that it does. It is also incredibly powerful. Bonhoeffer summarizes this power of confession:

When you confess your sin to another Christian . . . The expressed, acknowledged sin has lost all its power . . . He is no longer alone with his evil for he has cast off his sin in confession and handed it over to God. It has been taken away from him. Now he stands in the fellowship of sinners who live by the grace of God in the cross of Jesus Christ. Now he can be a sinner and still enjoy the grace of God. He can confess his sins and in this very act find fellowship for the first time. The sin concealed separated him from the fellowship, made all his apparent fellowship a sham; the sin confessed has helped him to find true fellowship with the brethren in Jesus Christ.[1]

Maybe you've needed to say this to someone for twenty years. Now is the time! No other community operates this way, but it is a remarkable hallmark of the people of God. Now, how the one who was wronged responds leads us to another critical aspect of practicing biblical community.

"I forgive you."

In May 1981 Pope John Paul was shot four times in an assassination attempt by Mehmet Ali Ağca during one of the pope's very typical outings in St. Peter's Square. The pope was critically wounded but survived, and Ağca was immediately imprisoned. Two years later, John Paul himself went to Ağca's prison and, in a stunning display that the world could not understand, *forgave* his would-be killer.

Perhaps the only thing more difficult for someone to do than admit that they are wrong, is to forgive someone who wronged them. This is precisely where the love of Christ is put on brilliant, irrefutable display in the Christian community. The only way that we will be able to practice forgiveness is in view of the cross. The gospel is that there was something so horribly wrong with each of us, that Jesus had to die for it. If Jesus had to die for the "wrong" in your friend, the odds of that "wrong" hurting you are probable. However, there can be no greater offense a person can commit against you than the thousands that you have committed against the Holy God of the Universe who has done nothing but love you perfectly. In the midst of our sin, we were perfectly loved, wholly forgiven, and rescued.

The only way you and I will be able to forgive someone who sins against us is if we remember that we are first sinners, and only second are we sinned against. We have been extended impossible, undeserved grace. And still, when someone sins against us, we have a tendency to jump into our judgment seat, demanding justice for the injustice committed against us. In the moment of intense pain or anger, we tend to develop spiritual amnesia and so easily forget that we are no better than the one that hurt us. If this person is a Christian, they even share in the same beautiful promise that you do. Paul tells us in Romans 8:1 "There is therefore now no condemnation for those who are in Christ Jesus." So as painful as it may be to unclench our fingers from around the gavel of judgment, as imitators of Christ, we cannot condemn where He does not.

So how does this work out? First we pray. Much like the "I'm sorry" statement, the "I forgive you" statement is only worth anything if it is true. The Bible uses the term *forgiveness* in debt collection terms. If you owe a debt, the debtor has the option to *forgive* your debt. If he/she forgives you, it means they agree to take the loss for you. They choose to suffer your penalty for you, and to consider you completely free from it. This is the biblical terminology used to describe what Christ did for us and what we are called to do for one another: to release all rights to punishing another for their transgression. To forgive is to release them from the debt you feel is owed by them for the pain they caused. We must take great care to come to a place where we can say "I forgive you" honestly and fully. The only way we get there is by making our home in the forgiveness given to us in Christ. We can then live believing God alone is judge and we are merely fellow sinners. A fellow sinner can only forgive in light of how much he or she has been forgiven.

The second step is where freedom enters in. If we are approached by a brother or sister who is confessing their sin, with humility we have the chance to speak *life* by saying something like, "As God forgave me, so I forgive you." What an honor for us to verbalize the great love of God to another!

Now, I warn you, resist the urge to simply dismiss the offense by saying, "It's okay." Sin is *never* okay. But it can be forgiven, and that is what we must communicate as God's people. Maybe you've been refusing forgiveness to one or multiple people for some time. Praise God, it is never too late to extend the grace of Christ to another.

"Christ is better."

Recently, a woman we'll call Cherie developed an unhealthy relationship with a man who lived overseas. The man was not a Christian, so I cannot really hold him to a Christian standard, but he was incredibly manipulative. Though he was dating other women, he still was trying to persuade Cherie to move across the world to be with him. Her small group had begged her to refuse, but she seemed blind to reason and set on going. Everyone in the group feared if she got on that plane she would harden her heart and fall away from following Christ.

The night she was supposed to leave, her small-group leader drove to her house with another in the group and confronted her. They took her passport and told her that though she couldn't see it right now, Christ was better than this relationship. They held the passport hostage because they couldn't get through to her. A short time later, Cherie e-mailed me with gratitude for her leaders, telling me their remarkable story.

You could probably summarize the entire letter to the Hebrews in the phrase "Christ is better." In Hebrews 3:12–13 the author summarizes how we are to put that truth into practice, saying

Take care, brothers, lest there be in any of you an evil, unbelieving heart, leading you to fall away from the living God. But exhort one another every day, as long as it is called "today," that none of you may be hardened by the deceitfulness of sin.

The author is reflecting back on the Israelites who would eventually harden their hearts to God Himself. Even though God had been with them, guiding them through the wilderness after He rescued them from Egypt, they still ended up being hardened to God's voice by the deceitfulness of sin. Here's another way to say it: Israel had blind spots. They had massive blind spots in their spiritual life and so do you. In our blindness, we believe that something will be better for us than what God has given to us. We believe that our ways are better than God's ways, and that the things of this earth will be more satisfying to us than God Himself. There in our self-deception is where we need to hear the beautiful truth that "Christ is better."

Many people react to the idea of opening up and being in community with incredulity. The general sentiment seems to be, "Really? What could I possibly get out of this? The people in my life aren't pastors or professional counselors— honestly, they're pretty screwed up. What credentials do any of these ordinary people have that would entice me to open up my life to them?" I'll tell you what their credentials are: *They are not you.* And there is a lot that any *not you* can see about *you* that *you* can't see. Have you ever heard your voice recorded and played back to you? What do you say? "Noooo, that's not what I sound like." And what does everyone around you say? "Yes, that's you." It's a fact nobody is immune from: we have blind spots.

How do we account for our blind spots? Very practically it means that you need to deputize some people to go hunting for sin in your life. You must leave your life completely open to them, and they need to commit to be as honest as necessary to point out the sin in your life. And here is the kicker: you commit to do the same for them; it's mutual.

Often, I've seen things like accountability groups get this one-third right. The people in these groups get up the courage to confess sin and say something like, "I've been looking at porn regularly for two weeks now." What a great moment! Confession! This is the part they get right.

Now, in that heavy formative moment for the confessor, *what is our response*? This is the part most accountability groups get wrong. I've heard more times than I can count something like, "That's rough man, we're glad you told us." Or I've seen groups force guys to pay five dollars to help them feel like the sin cost them something. What the confessor needs is not sympathy or punishment; what the confessor needs is Christ. He needs someone to look him in the eyes as Christ's representative and say, "Christ is better than ____." He needs to be reminded of the gospel that he chose to disbelieve in some form or fashion in his sin.

For example, many view porn as a way to find escape from reality. What promises escape, actually imprisons them more to the need for porn to feel escape. Like all addicts, their escape becomes their prison. They were designed to find rest in Christ. They need to see they've traded Christ for porn. They need to see that they are saying with their lives, "Christ is not better." Someone needs to look such a man or woman in the eye and say out loud, "You've traded Christ for porn and it will never deliver for you. Christ is so much better. He forgives you and He can rescue you. Let's fight this together."

Do you have that kind of fellowship with anybody? Someone you sit down face-to-face with and allow them to inspect your life? To watch your mannerisms and see your facial expressions? You need someone who will put a hand on your shoulder and pray the promises of Scripture over you as you rip off your mask and expose the ugly in your life, who can look you in the eye and say, "Christ is better!" Maybe now is the time to start practicing this in your life.

"How can I serve you?"

One of our small-group leaders told me recently about a woman in her group who had one of those lightbulb moments where it clicked for her regarding how Christ serving her should create a readiness to serve others. Later that month the group learned of a refugee family who had moved into our city with nothing but the clothes on their backs. Within 24 hours, the girl had taken her own bed to the refugees' apartment (which another family in the church had found for them). The woman slept on her floor with joy until she followed God overseas to take the gospel to where no one has heard it yet.

The depiction of Christ in Scripture defies so many expectations of what a king should be. He is a servant. Jesus said of Himself in Matthew 20:28, *"The Son of Man came not to be served but to serve, and to give his life as a ransom for many."* Christ is summarizing the good news as one coming to serve all so that all may live. The New Testament Church is to assume the disposition of serving one another. Paul says in Galatians 5:13, "For you were called to freedom, brothers. Only do not use your freedom as an opportunity for the flesh, but through love serve one another." Paul's comment *through love* is drawing on the gospel where Christ served us in love. So when we serve, we are displaying Christ to one another. Serving one another should be something we *get* to do, not something we are *guilted* to do.

Christ's love frees us to be humble enough to serve and empowers us to do so with joy. What does this look like? This one probably takes on the most varied of forms out of all of these starter phrases. The idea behind it is simply that as Christ served you, so you also want to serve another.

"I love you."

A frustrated husband once asked me why his wife doubted his love for her, saying, "I said 'I love you' when I married her and nothing has changed!" We often assume love in relationships, although love is designed to be expressed. The family of Christ is no exception. A part of embodying the love of Christ for us is verbalizing it!

Think about the power of the phrase *I love you*. Some reading this have not said this to anyone in years. Maybe this is because no one said it to you. But the God of the universe has spoken His love loudly, clearly, and irrefutably over you in the gospel. This is John 3:16, that God so loved the world (read: you and me) that He gave His son. That is not just love demonstrated, but words written by John to you so you would hear your Father's love for you. So we should begin verbalizing our love as we demonstrate it. When you do, I want you to try the following:

- eye contact
- not laughing
- audible (don't mumble this away)

For some this may be the best marriage training you've had in a while! But this phrase is also intended for use within the family of God. I've gotten into this habit with some of the guys I know well, and it is an affirming practice. We don't say it all of the time, but we say it enough that we don't run the risk of just assuming it.

How do you work this in? It's going to be awkward at first. You should start with people you are close enough to that this would not be out of place. And you are looking for moments that carry enough weight for it to not be perceived as casual.

For example: when I saw a friend recently who moved away a couple of years ago, we said, "I love you, man" before parting ways again.

First John 4:19 says, "We love because he first loved us." So if you have trouble getting those words out of your mouth *honestly*, then you need only to look back to the cross, because one who understands how greatly he is loved will be able to love others.

Use these starter phrases like training wheels. Hopefully you will get to the point where gospeling one another becomes a natural part of your language, and you will not need a set of phrases anymore. In fact, you will probably develop nuanced ways of speaking the love of Christ deeply into your own context.

SOME OBSTACLES TO GOSPELING ONE ANOTHER

While this sounds great in theory, there are a few things that can keep you from implementing a healthy gospeling practice into your community of believers. Here are two that we've found to be the biggest obstacles.

Margin

While writing this chapter, I received two text messages from two guys in my small group. One asked if he could come over in a couple of hours after my kids went to bed to talk through some questions raised in a recent conversation he had with a non-Christian. A few minutes later, another guy asked if we could get a few minutes on the phone or in person to talk through a dating relationship he's in. Back when we started our small group together, we all made an agreement to do life with one another. That sounded wonderful the day that we started our group, but on nights like the one I'm describing, the extra demands on my time can feel overwhelming.

I've got kids, ministry, and how can I have time for community when I'm trying to write a book about it? Actually, these guys understand that perfectly. And they are incredibly gracious with me in the midst of my chaotic life. But, we made an agreement to reach out to one another and to be available when reached out to. These guys are honoring the commitment we made to be an intentional part of each other's lives—even when, *especially* when, the rest of life is busy. And I do the same to them often. The only way I'm able to say yes to these spur-of-the-moment requests is because my wife, Courtney, and I have fought hard to build margin into our lives. We have intentionally left some space between what we *could* commit to and what we *will* commit to. That is because we know spiritually formative moments often do not happen in our living room between seven and nine at our Sunday-night small group, but rather in the informal one-on-one conversations that spin off of those gatherings. A lack of margin in your life can be one of the biggest obstacles to gospeling one another.

Are you living your life with any margin? That is, do you have time and space to respond when someone you are trying to "do life with" seeks you out? The way we communicate this idea to our small group is that the calendar should serve us, we should not serve our calendar. A good friend who is a small-group leader at the Summit calls this "logging hours" with his group. He tells his group that quality time requires quantity time.

Ultimately this obstacle is a matter of priorities. Where do the people of God stack up in your priorities? Are they a meeting on your calendar or the people that you do life with? We must build our calendars around our relationships, not the other way around.

Here is a simple way to start overcoming this obstacle: do things together—sometimes.

Take a look at the rhythms of your life. The regular activities you do, the errands you run, and even your dinner schedule. Consider how you can incorporate your community of believers into some of those. For me, I rarely go to a hardware store without Jeremy. Our family rarely goes a week without one or two single people from our group joining us for family dinner. Now, my introverted readers can calm down. You don't *always* have to do things together.

The idea here is not to have more things on your calendar, but to invite others into some things you are already doing anyway.

Fear

For most people, having meaningful conversations is a daunting task. We live in a world that conditions us to be relationally risk averse. For example, if a guy is too scared to ask a girl out, he can utilize the cowardly crutch of social media to message her, then text her, and then pull what I have unaffectionately termed the "group-outing-sneak-a-date" move. He can do many things to avoid looking her in the eye and expressing an interest in her, even though that's the only thing she should respond to if her father has taught her well. (You'll have to forgive me, I'm a new daddy of daughters, and any former passion about this subject has quadrupled since those precious little girls came into my life.)

The point is, we are afraid to become transparent with one another because when we do, it makes us vulnerable. Vulnerability is many things, but it is always a risk. Men especially tend to shy away from vulnerability and treat the whole idea as if it's antimasculine. The notion that transparency is somehow distinctly feminine is a dangerous lie. To be transparent is to reveal our true self to another person. I'm not talking about a cryfest here, but about a genuine verbalized reflection on how you interpret the circumstances and relationships in your life. Remember, the person you will be talking to is a broken sinner just like you. So if your heart is racing and the predominant question in your mind is, "What will they think of me?" . . . well, who cares? Your friend's job is simply to tell you what Jesus thinks of you, and that has been decidedly declared in the gospel. Do not let fear of man rob you from the great joy God has given you in the gift of transparent relationships with other Christians.

Here's a way to start overcoming this obstacle: go first. The only way to break down fear and build up trust is to believe the gospel, then from there start trying. Maybe start putting this entire chapter into practice by reading it together as a small group and then agreeing to be transparent with someone in the group over the course of the next week. This transparency will begin to allow your group to fight sin *with* one another. You can begin to fight a battle together you were never intended to fight alone anyway.

Maybe you simply need to offer a little deeper look into your own life during your next group discussion. Whatever you do, especially if you are leading the group, the group will most likely follow. You set the bar for how open and trustworthy your group will be. Go for it. If they reject you, then you will simply be closer to the image of the Christ whose approval is the only one you need.

DISCUSSION QUESTIONS

1. How does gospeling one another improve community?

2. What aspect of gospeling one another seems the most daunting?

3. What aspect of gospeling one another seems the most beneficial?

CHAPTER 7

GOSPEL FLOW

When the church tries to bottle up the Spirit within
herself, she acts contrary both to her own and to his
nature. For it is the nature of the church to be ever
enlarging her borders, and it is the nature of the
Spirit to transmit His life to ever-widening circles.
When the church does not recognize this law of her
being and of the being of the Spirit, the Spirit is
quenched and he withdraws himself, and the deposit
of religiosity that is left becomes a putrification in
the lives of those who have grieved him.

HENRY BOER

The unity of the Trinity is constituted by the Father,
concentrated round the Son, and illumined through
the Holy Spirit.... To throw open the circulatory move-
ment of the divine light and the divine relationships,
and to take men and women, with the whole of cre-
ation, into the life-stream of the triune God: that is the
meaning of creation, reconciliation and glorification.

JÜRGEN MOLTMANN

STAGNANT

One of my life goals is to survive in the wilderness and kill a bear. I know this sounds crazy, but ever since college I have had this yearning for an experience like Anthony Hopkins had in his movie *The Edge*. Say it with me, "We will kill the bear!" For several years I have planned and prepared for this adventure. I once even took a survival class. I expected the bulk of survival 101 to be spent on the ins and outs of making rope, fashioning spears, learning to kill, climb, and conquer! But, much to my surprise, the class mostly focused around one topic: water.

Our bodies can survive a week without food, but they can't go more than a day or two without water. So, naturally, one of the primary elements to surviving the wild is learning to find, gather, and clean water. I learned that water can be found in some pretty crazy places, but I also learned that not all water is healthy to drink. Because of this, the instructor made us repeat a mantra over and over again: "Dead water equals dead people."

When looking for water, it is vital to always search for places where the water is not stagnant. You see, stagnant water has significantly lower oxygen, which gives way to dangerous things like bacteria and larvae. You recognize a stagnant source of water by the horrible stench or aroma it puts off. Flowing water, however, has a continual source of oxygen, which keeps the water more free from harmful elements, making it a safe place from which to draw.

Have you ever sat in church or in your small group and wondered, "Why does this feel so dead?" Most of us who have spent extended amounts of time in or around the church have had these moments that make us ask ourselves, "Is this it?" The instruction that continually comes up in the early church of the New Testament is, "Go!" Don't just stay there. Make disciples. Put your hand to the plow and don't look back. Keep moving forward.

In consulting with churches on how to build toward biblical community, I am constantly surprised by the segmented gospel many pastors have built into the minds and hearts of their people. A ministry structure communicates this when there is higher priority given to connection to a church program over deep relationships. When there is more time spent branding the program than training the lay leaders, it's a wonder why there is shock at the shallow outcomes. We may exalt the righteous desire for people to immerse themselves in the deep waters of biblical community, but all we have put before them is a kiddy pool or shallow creek. The problem is not that our people are not willing to go deep, but that we've given them shallow water. As pastors we have the privilege and responsibility to shepherd our people toward maturity in Christ. Our ability to do this is only as limited as our understanding of the gospel. A church where the gospel is stagnant will always have the stench of death. A community where the gospel is static is not a source of life.

GETTING THE STORY STRAIGHT

Narratives have captivated mankind's attention since the beginning of time. Plato, Socrates, Shakespeare, C. S. Lewis, J. R. R Tolkien, and Dostoyevsky all tap into the human love of story. Why? Because story is a powerful tool. Through story, we are moved to do things beyond the ordinary.

The Christian metanarrative, the gospel, is the central story to all human history.

Therefore remember that at one time you Gentiles in the flesh, called "the uncircumcision" by what is called the circumcision, which is made in the flesh by hands—remember that you were at that time separated from Christ, alienated from the commonwealth of Israel and strangers to the covenants of promise, having no hope and without God in the world. But now in Christ Jesus you who once were far off have been brought near by the blood of Christ. For he himself is our peace, who has made us both one and has broken down in his flesh the dividing wall of hostility by abolishing the law of commandments expressed in ordinances, that he might create in himself one new man in place of the two, so making peace, and might reconcile us both to God in one body through the cross, thereby killing the hostility. And he came and preached peace to you who were far off and peace to those who were near. For through him we both have access in one Spirit to the Father. So then you are no longer strangers and aliens, but you are fellow citizens with the saints and members of the household of God. (Eph. 2:11–22)

Through Christ, God redeems and reconciles a people to Himself. He takes those whom the book of Ephesians calls dead, estranged, lost, and alienated and grafts them into the grand gospel story, making them adopted sons and daughters in the family of God. In the gospel, we see a clear picture of how we are not only brought from death to life, but have also been brought into a movement. As believers we were not only rescued out of our sad story, one filled with bondage to sin and death, but we are woven into God's redemptive story. Paul writes that when God reconciles us to Himself, He calls us out of death and darkness into life and light. He makes those who were once strangers and aliens sons and daughters.

God does not enter into our story. He grafts us into the grand story of redemption that has been unfolding, a story of a loving God redeeming and reconciling a people to Himself. If this is your story, then you have a powerful tool to paint a picture of freedom for everyone around you. You and I were once far from God, dead in our sins and trespasses, and without hope. But God, being rich in His mercy and love, reconciled us to Himself through Christ. We have been set free by the blood of the cross; you and I no longer live, but Christ lives within us.

Biblical community is a tapestry of freedom stories. Individually, these stories speak of a loving God who uniquely intervened and brought us out of darkness and into His marvelous light. Corporately, they put on display the grand epic that God is telling. As a dear friend shared with me, the spiritual family is one where we are welcomed to the table, but the focus is not us; the focus is Jesus—He is the centerpiece. You see, the gospel shifts the paradigm of what it means to relate and belong to one another. In the spiritual family, what binds us together is no longer socioeconomic status, race, ethnicity, affinity, or geography. The gospel is what links the members of the spiritual family together.

When I first began pastoring small groups, I had an encounter that solidified this idea for me and changed the way I shepherd people into biblical community. At an event where those looking to connect into group life come, meet group leaders in their areas, and ideally join a group, I saw, out of the corner of my eye, a man standing by himself, looking disoriented. I walked up to him to see if I could help him find a group. He sharply replied, "You don't have what I need here!" Revealing the issue, he said, "You don't have the type of community I need." He then began to list all the things that made up his idea of community: a group that met on Friday nights, a group that provided child care, a group with men his age, a group that wasn't going to require any reading or preparation. On and on the list went. I politely told him that he was right: based on those criteria, there wasn't a group that was going to fit his needs. Sadly, his expectations for community were not informed or shaped by the gospel—just his felt needs.

The problem wasn't that we did not offer a wide enough variety of groups for people to peruse. The problem was that in order to faithfully shepherd people into community, we needed to set the story straight from the beginning. We now begin every connecting event by bringing everyone together in one room to inform their expectations of community theologically. "It's okay to be wounded and broken . . ."

We were created for community. That longing deep inside us to belong to something bigger than ourselves is a part of our creational DNA. The lie of sin is that we don't need one another and that we can be autonomous, self-sufficient Christians, and the culture around us incites this way of thinking. At the end of the day, we want to be the heroes of our stories. We want to believe that this life is all about us. What this man needed wasn't a group that met all of his consumeristic expectations; he needed to be confronted with the reality that community isn't simply an optional additive to the Christian life. Community for the believer isn't an issue of programmatic preference, but of biblical faithfulness. Paul David Tripp emphasizes our need for community when he says, "We are incessant interpreters of our own realities, coupled with the fact that we lack plausible deniability with ourselves. We need each other to consistently communicate the truth of where we stand with sin and God to us in a way that penetrates our delusions."[1]

Shepherding people toward community means setting the story straight from the beginning. The gospel is the tie that binds biblical community together. The gospel means that you and I have been set free from the bondage of Satan, sin, and death and have been brought into the glorious light of freedom in Christ. Whatever defined our lives prior to Christ no longer does because we have a great story to tell. Gospel-centered community happens when we are lovingly confronted with the reality that our life is not our own, it was bought with a price. The grace that purchased our freedom wasn't cheap, it was costly grace. As the song says, "This grace bids I come and die that I might live!" The gospel is the form and substance of biblical community.

GOSPEL FLOW

The gospel isn't stagnant, but flowing.

From now on, therefore, we regard no one according to the flesh. Even though we once regarded Christ according to the flesh, we regard him thus no longer. Therefore, if anyone is in Christ, he is a new creation. The old has passed away; behold, the new has come. All this is from God, who through Christ reconciled us to himself and gave us the ministry of reconciliation; that is, in Christ God was reconciling the world to himself, not counting their trespasses against them, and entrusting to us the message of reconciliation. Therefore, we are ambassadors for Christ, God making his appeal through us. We implore you on behalf of Christ, be reconciled to God. For our sake he made him to be sin who knew no sin, so that in him we might become the righteousness of God. (2 Cor. 5:16–21)

Some time ago my wife and I took a trip to Israel, where I noticed something profound—a great picture of 2 Corinthians. In Israel, the north is significantly different from the south.

Right in the middle of the northern territory is the Sea of Galilee. Running across the country from north to south is the Jordan River. The Jordan runs into the north end of Galilee. All around this body of water is lush farmland and beautiful weather. As you follow the Jordan, it flows into the Sea of Galilee and out, heading south. As you move farther south, the landscape gradually becomes dry, arid desert running right into the Dead Sea. This area is void of life because the Jordan River ends there—the Dead Sea consumes it, and there is no outflow. The flow of the river terminates in the Dead Sea, creating a stagnant space with no growth whatsoever. It doesn't breathe life into its surroundings; it consumes life.

Laying 2 Corinthians over this imagery, we see that the gospel has a flowing nature to it. The gospel comes in and reconciles us to God, but the gospel also goes out as we become messengers of reconciliation. Through Christ we are reconciled to God and made messengers on mission. When the gospel isn't expressed in and through our lives and the message of redemption terminates in us, it creates a vacuum of life. When we do not understand the full picture— *this fluid nature of the gospel*—we are led to a stagnant, complacent Christianity.

We know that community is not the goal—growing into the image of Christ is the goal—but community is the vehicle by which we move toward the goal. Community provides the ideal context for the gospel to flow in and flow out. When the gospel does not flow in and through your community, your groups will become vessels for consumerism rather than ones that give life.

GOSPEL IN, GOSPEL OUT

Gospel-centered community is a radical call amid a culture of mere attendance and casual involvement. It involves mutual love, care, consistency, and authenticity as we seek to adore the person and work of Christ with our lives. Where these elements are lacking, we have moved away from gospel-centered community and into the realm of social clubs. As Bonhoeffer describes it, "the people of God are bearers of the gospel to one another."[2]

Though this type of community can be expressed in various ways, there are particular practices that the Bible commands for healthy functioning of the body. These commands demonstrate fruit from the gospel flowing into a people, that through Christ, we are reconciled to God and to one another. This defines the function of how we exist together. We are to love one another (John 13:34), outdo one another in showing honor (Rom. 12:10), live in harmony with one another (Rom. 12:16), comfort and agree with one another (2 Cor. 13:11), serve one another (Gal. 5:13), bear one another's burdens (Gal. 6:2), forgive one another (Eph. 4:32), submit to one another (Eph. 5:21), be honest with one another (Col. 3:9), encourage one another (1 Thess. 5:11), confess to and pray for one another (James 5:16), and humble ourselves before one another (1 Pet. 5:5). How can we carry out these obligations toward one another if we do not know and love one another? The gospel is not merely a story of salvation from something; it is also our account of being saved into something.

The Bible says that the old has passed away, and the new has come. Then it says that, through Christ, God reconciled us to Himself and gave us the ministry of reconciliation. This takes place in community. Community is a conduit and a canvas for the gospel to be poured out and displayed to the lost and dying world around us—for mission. Mission does not come before the gospel; it comes because of the gospel. The love of Christ compels us. A community engaging in mission out of anything other than a response to the gospel is at best advocacy. When the gospel lands and blows up group life, you have an overflow of gospel-centered living that flows out, permeating neighborhoods, schools, softball teams, and on and on. Community life also has a distinct opportunity to herald Christ by how we interact with one another. Our society is saturated with the lie that everything is about you. Community is a place where this paradigm can be transformed. It is a place where it can be redeemed with a full, accurate, and fluid picture of the gospel of Jesus Christ.

GOSPEL MISSION

*I have manifested your name to the people whom you gave me out of the world. Yours they were, and you gave them to me, and they have kept your word. Now they know that everything that you have given me is from you. For I have given them the words that you gave me, and they have received them and have come to know in truth that I came from you; and they have believed that you sent me. I am praying for them. I am not praying for the world but for those whom you have given me, for they are yours. All mine are yours, and yours are mine, and I am glorified in them. And I am no longer in the world, but they are in the world, and I am coming to you. Holy Father, keep them in your name, which you have given me, that **they may be one,** even **as we are one.** While I was with them, I kept them in your name, which you have given me. I have guarded them, and not one of them has been lost except the son of destruction, that the Scripture might be fulfilled. But now I am coming to you, and these things I speak in the world, that they may have my joy* *fulfilled in themselves. I have given them your word, and the world has hated them because they are not of the world, just as I am not of the world. I do not ask that you take them out of the world, but that you keep them from the evil one. They are not of the world, just as I am not of the world. Sanctify them in the truth; your word is truth. As you **sent me** into the world, so I have **sent them** into the world. And for their sake I consecrate myself, that they also may be sanctified in truth.* (John 17:6–19, emphasis added)

The people of God are a sent people. One of the most significant ways we can be missional in group life is in the continual raising up and sending out of people from within our community to multiply gospel efforts across the city. We rightly reflect our divine communal image when we replicate for the world what God has done for us in Christ. In the community of the Trinity, we see God displaying His love by *sending* the Son to redeem and reconcile a fallen creation back to Himself. Through Christ, we have been made vessels for this message of reconciliation and sent out.

In the conversation on discipleship, community is often elevated as the goal. Community is not the goal but rather the vehicle that God has designed for His people to pursue sanctification together. Mission is the engine that drives this vehicle. We cannot separate mission from community in the conversation of discipleship.

DISCIPLESHIP

COMMUNITY

MISSION

We must derive our philosophy and strategy from a theological foundation. Here we see Jesus setting the construct for His people to reflect the image of the triune God to the world. This affects not only how we relate to one another (gospel in) but also how we relate to the world (gospel out). When building discipleship in group life, the matrix we always have to come back to is what Jesus prayed for the Church, that we would be a people transformed by the gospel, unified through the gospel, and sent with the gospel.

Jesus talks about how important this framework is to Christian community in John 13:34–35:

A new commandment I give to you, that you love one another: just as I have loved you, you also are to love one another. By this all people will know that you are my disciples, if you have love for one another.

Love is the dearest and deepest mark of a Christian. Love is not only evidence of a disciple, it is the framework for much of what God commands the Church to be and do. The Christian community is designed to be a tangible picture of the gospel to the world through how we love one another. A community of people transformed by the gospel is a distinctly loving people.

A few years ago I (Trevor) was walking in an extended season of exhaustion. I felt tired, far from the Lord, and ineffective in ministry. I had been walking in a season where life just seemed to speed past me and I could never quite catch up. I thought if I could just get alone, then I could get a greater bearing on what was going on in my own heart and life. When your household consists of multiple kids below the age of five in minimum square footage, quiet time isn't a currency that flows in abundance. That year my wife and I had the opportunity to get away to a cabin with some dear friends on a sort of retreat. I had a picture in my mind of a good book, a cup of coffee, and nothing to interrupt me. My thought was, "If I can only get alone, I might find that rich time with the Lord I've been longing for."

On the first morning the smell of coffee and warm breakfast filled the room, and we gathered around the table to eat before setting off on our individual journeys. What came next wasn't the eat-and-run experience I had in mind. I wasn't looking for fellowship, but quite the opposite. I was hoping to get alone, slow life down so I could grab the reins, and get a handle on this runaway carriage. Just moments into the meal I realized my longing wasn't to be alone, but to be present in what God was doing among us over a meal. We laughed and cried while we shared stories of where we were in life, both the bad and the good.

This wasn't the first meal I had shared with friends, but what God refreshed in my heart around that table was the deep fellowship that we can have with one another when He is the reason we gather. Amid our hectic pace of life, I lost sight of something precious—a means of grace given to the people of God to gather and reflect on His goodness and provision. The love of Christ uniquely shapes how we interact with one another.

I need community, a group of people committed to seeing me look more like Jesus. When we aren't diligent to fight for that, our fingers grip the things of this world tighter, and our affections drift from the Creator to the creation.

Tim Chester talks about drift in this way:

> Our problem is that we think of ourselves as being the center of our world. We think of our lives as a story, and if we're Christians, as God being one of the characters in the story. We look for Him when we need Him and expect Him to be grateful when we serve Him. He's a lovely piece of our story, but we still think of it as our story. But it's not our story. It's God's story.[3]

Community is a means of grace by which God uses the body to reorient our mind's attention and our heart's affection back to Him. God's people have gathered to break bread together and to adore Him together since the very beginning. For the follower of Christ, a meal is a precious opportunity to invite others into our lives. A meal involves welcoming, creating space, listening, and providing. In his book *A Meal with Jesus*, Tim Chester says, "Meals slow things down. . . . Meals force you to be people oriented instead of task oriented. . . . It's possible to remain at a distance from someone in public gatherings. . . . Meals bring you close."[4]

We all come to the idea of community with our own anxieties and expectations, but around the table of fellowship we can experience Christ anew. This is the epicenter of gospel mission. A people gathering together to celebrate what the Lord has done and to cultivate in one another lives that reflect gospel transformation.

We say often that one of the most significant ways a group can be missional is to be intentional about planting new groups closer to where people live so that they might be able to walk in community where life exists. This closer proximity allows for the rhythms of the individual lives in that group to intersect more frequently. One of our goals is to have a group within walking distance of every person that attends our church. We want to see neighborhoods saturated with communities where the gospel is being lived in and through that group to the lost world around them. A group where the gospel is being lived out and discipleship is happening will have a ripple effect in the place where it exists. When those communities are living out the gospel among one another, they are demonstrating it to the world around them.

"It is our cross-love for each other that proclaims the truth of the gospel to a watching and skeptical world. Our love for one another, to the extent that it imitates and conforms to the cross-love of Jesus for us, is evangelistic . . . Too much evangelism is an attempt to answer questions people are not asking. Let them experience the life of the

Christian community. . . . Let our relationships provoke questions."[5]

We started this chapter by asking if you have ever sat in church or in your small group and wondered, "Why does this feel so dead?" I have spoken with many pastors who are frustrated at the lack of evangelistic fervor in their group ministries. The answer to this question comes in our understanding of gospel flow. The depth to which the gospel has impacted a community will absolutely determine the gospel reach of that community. Stagnant communities are those who have lost focus on the reason they are gathering. They're stagnant because the gospel doesn't make its way out of their group but rather terminates in them. Symptoms of this kind of community tend to be marked by comments such as:

- "The men in my group keep confessing the same sin week in and week out without any change."
- "I can't seem to get people in our group to follow up with one another during the week."
- "On nights that we are taking up a collection to help a ministry in need everyone contributes, but when we are having a work day in our neighborhood most of the people in our group are conveniently busy."

These phrases and more are ones that we hear over and over again in group life. What they illustrate is that the spiritual growth of that group has hit a ceiling and become stagnant. There might be numerous solutions to deploy to address each of these situations specifically, but they are symptoms of a larger problem, a gospel problem. The gospel means we are set free from death and into life and light. In group life, gospel depth equals gospel impact.

In building toward gospel-centered group life, we have to set as the foundation, the message and the mission. The gospel informs not only how I live my life, but how we interact with one another and the world. "For the kingdom of God does not consist in talk but in power" (1 Cor. 4:20). Discipleship in group life happens when we are consistently seeing the Christ formed in us and proclaimed through us in power.

DISCUSSION QUESTIONS

1. Currently, how is the gospel flow of your community?
2. How can you improve the gospel flow of your community moving forward?

AFTERWORD

The story is told of a young pastor discouraged by the relatively small size of his congregation. An older mentor, knowing of the struggle, wrote him: "I know you are discouraged that your congregation is considerably smaller than those under the care of some of your friends. But believe me, when you stand before God and give account for the souls committed to your care, as Holy Scripture tells us we must, the weight of souls under your care will be more than enough."

As a pastor, I often tremble in thinking about the accountability I have to pastor people well. Pastoring is more than growing an audience; it is shepherding people, *watching* over their souls.

Long ago I came to realize that I simply could not look after more than a couple dozen people well. So if I am to pastor responsibly, I must raise up other pastors and leaders who watch over the flock with me. Spence Shelton was just such a gift of God to me. I have told him—somewhat lightheartedly, and somewhat deadly serious—that when God asks me to give an account for the people of the Summit Church, I am going to ask him to come stand beside me. I imagine he would then turn to the leaders, and leaders *of* leaders, that he has trained here, so that they might stand beside us to help us give account. We are attempting to pastor our people well, and we do this not by restricting the size of our church, but by multiplying pastors.

This is the way Paul says it should be. "What you have heard from me in the presence of many witnesses entrust to faithful men who will be able to teach others also" (2 Tim 2:2). The heart of the Great Commission is leadership development.

Leadership development has been Spence's forte at our church. He has overseen those small group "pastors" who are the first line of ministry for those in our congregation. We believe that discipleship happens in relationships, not just from listening to sermons, because leaders intimately involved with people can apply the Word more specifically than I can cover from the pulpit.

We often conceptualize our complementary roles as "air war" and "ground war." In a weekend message, I am the air war, "carpet-bombing" (as it were) the congregation with the Word. Air war is a crucial part of any occupation campaign, but military strategists agree that air war can never suffi- ciently drive out an enemy. Air war merely paves the way for ground war. Infantry must root the enemy out of the holes and caves they have dug into the ground. Our small group leaders are our ground war, helping to apply the Word to broken areas in the lives of our people in ways I cannot do from the pulpit.

We execute almost everything at our church on the small group level. It is in small groups that we empower for evangelism, that we hold people accountable, that we inculcate spiritual disciplines, that we develop mentoring relationships. In small groups, the Spirit is at work—exposing sin and knitting the body together in love and community. In small groups, we mobilize our people to minister to the brokenness of our community. We even send out many short-term mission trips through small groups. In other words, *in small groups, we make disciples.*

Small groups are not independent churches, but they function in many ways as a microcosm of the larger body.

I can think of few people who lead in this ministry initiative as well as Spence Shelton. I am grateful for the service he has personally provided to the Summit Church, and has now provided for the larger church through this book—equipping others to equip the saints for the work of the ministry.

J.D. Greear

NOTES

Chapter 1

1. John Piper, "Marks of a Spiritual Leader," http://www.desiringgod.org/resource-library/books/the-marks-of-a-spiritual-leader.

2. Norman Grubb, *C. T. Studd: Cricketer and Pioneer* (1933; repr., Fort Washington, PA: CLC Publications, 2008).

3. Greg Somerville, "Take This Group and Own It!," in *Why Small Groups?: Together toward Maturity*, ed. C. J. Mahaney (Gaithersburg, MD: Sovereign Grace Ministries, 1996), 35.

4. Geoff Ashley, "Picture of a Shepherd," The Village Church, http://www.thevillagechurch.net/sermon/the-picture -of-a-shepherd/.

5. Dietrich Bonhoeffer, *Life Together* (New York: Harper & Row, 1954), 23.

6. Timothy J. Keller, *Gospel in Life Discussion Guide with DVD: Grace Changes Everything* (Grand Rapids: Zondervan, 2010).

7. Tim Chester and Steve Timmis, *Total Church: A Radical Reshaping around Gospel and Community*, North American ed. (Wheaton, IL: Crossway Books, 2008).

8. J. Oswald Sanders, *Spiritual Leadership: A Commitment to Excellence*, 2nd rev. ed. (Chicago: Moody, 1994), 28.

9. Tim Chester, *You Can Change* (Wheaton, IL: Crossway, 2010), 106.

Chapter 2

1. A. W. Tozer, *The Knowledge of the Holy* (New York: HarperCollins, 1961), 17.

2. Bruce A. Ware, *Father, Son, and Holy Spirit: Relationships, Roles, and Relevance* (Wheaton, IL: Crossway Books, 2005), 156. Much of the thought in this chapter was influenced by chapter 6 of Ware's book. While his applications focus more on authority and submission in Christian relationships than ours, his theological insight into the Trinity was helpful and we commend it to you.

3. "Westminster Confession of Faith: Modern English Study Version," Chapter 2, ¶3, "God and the Holy Trinity." The historic Nicene Creed and more recently the Baptist Faith & Message also summarize the Trinity in an accessible fashion.

4. Philip Graham Ryken and Michael LeFebvre, *Our Triune God: Living in the Love of the Three-in-One* (Wheaton, IL: Crossway, 2011), 92.

5. Ware, *Father, Son, and Holy Spirit*, 134, emphasis added.

6. **The People of God** (1 Pet. 2:10); **The Family** (Eph. 3; 2 Cor. 6:18; 1 John 2; and many references by Paul to the church as "brothers."); **The Body** (1 Cor. 12:12–27); **Bride of Christ** (2 Cor. 11:2; Eph. 5); **A Holy Priesthood** (2 Pet. 2:5); **Branches on a Vine** (John 15:1–8); **Field of Crops and a Building** (1 Cor. 3:6–9; Hebrews 3:2–6); **A New Temple** (1 Pet. 2:5); **Pillar of Truth** (1 Tim. 3:15).

7. C. S. Lewis, *Mere Christianity* rev. ed. (New York: HarperCollins, 2009), 165.

8. Dietrich Bonhoeffer, *Life Together* (New York: Harper & Row, 1954), 27–28.

9. Francis Schaeffer, *The Mark of a Christian*, 2nd ed. (Downers Grove, IL: InterVarsity, 2006), 29.

10. Ed Stetzer, Richie Stanley, and Jason Hayes, *Lost & Found: The Younger Unchurched and the Churches that Reach Them* (Nashville: B&H, 2009), 65. In the particular survey cited, "young-unchurched" represents the twenty- to twenty-nine-year-old age range of those not attending a church.

11. Another helpful read in this vein is *Total Church* by Tim Chester and Steve Timmis.

Chapter 3

1. Quoted from Matthew 12:46–50. Also found in Mark 3:31–35 and Luke 8:19–21.

2. John Piper, "Single in Christ: A Name Better Than Sons and Daughters" (online sermon, Desiring God Ministry, April 29, 2007), http://www.desiringgod.org/sermons/single-in-christ-a-name-better-than-sons-and-daughters. This idea of the "primacy" of the family of God comes from John Piper's sermon.

Chapter 4

1. Matt Chandler, Josh Patterson, and Eric Geiger, *Creature of the Word: The Jesus-Centered Church* (Nashville: B&H, 2012).

2. Peter M. Senge, *The Fifth Discipline* (New York: Currency/Doubleday, 1990), 155, quoted in Andy Stanley, *Next Generation Leader: Five Essentials for Those Who Will Shape the Future* (Colorado Springs: Multnomah, 2003), 71.

3. Stanley, *Next Generation*, 73.

Chapter 5

1. Larry Osborne wrote an excellent brief article, "Seven Advantages of Sermon-Based Small Groups," where you can find more of his insights on the sermon-based approach. The article is available online at http://www.smallgroups.com/articles/2008/sevenadvantagesofsermonbasedsmallgroups.html.

2. Patrick Lencioni, *The Advantage: Why Organizational Health Trumps Everything Else in Business* (San Francisco: Jossey-Bass, 2012).

3. Thom S. Rainer and Eric Geiger, *Simple Church: Returning to God's Process for Making Disciples* (Nashville: B&H, 2011).

Chapter 6

1. Bonhoeffer, *Life Together*, 112–13.

Chapter 7

1. Tripp, *Instruments in the Redeemers Hands*.

2. Bonhoeffer, *Life Together*.

3. Chester, *You Can Change*, 106.

4. Tim Chester, *A Meal with Jesus* (Wheaton, IL: Crossway, 2011), 47.

5. Tim Chester and Steve Timmis, *Total Church* (Wheaton, IL: Crossway Books, 2008), 57–59.